THE **SCIENCE OF READING** IN PRACTICE

STEPHANIE STOLLAR
& KATE WINN

READING ASSESSMENT DONE RIGHT

Tools and Techniques for Data-Driven Instruction

DEDICATION

To teachers everywhere, entrusted with the profound and beautiful responsibility of unlocking the power of reading for every child.

Senior Vice President and Publisher: Tara Welty
Executive Editorial Director: Sarah Longhi
Editor-in-Chief: Raymond Coutu
Production Editor: Danny Miller
Assistant Editor: Samantha Unger
Cover design: Tannaz Fassihi
Interior design: Maria Lilja

Photo credits: Cover photos © Getty Images and Shutterstock.com. Classroom photos courtesy of Kate Winn, Kari Bowles, and Brandi Wagner/Clarity with Grace Photography. Author photos courtesy of Ali Herlihey Photography and Brandi Wagner/Clarity with Grace Photography.

Credits: 32: "Oral Reading Fluency" graphic by Speechy Musings. Copyright © Speechy Musings. Reprinted by permission; 46: "The Collaborative Improvement Cycle" graphic from *MTSS for Reading Improvement: A Leader's Tool Kit for Schoolwide Success* by Sarah Brown and Stephanie Stollar. Copyright © 2025 by Solution Tree Press. Used with permission; 63, 65, 66, 69, 73, 74, 76, 93, 94, 112 Forms: "First Sound Fluency BOY Grade K," "Phoneme Segmentation Fluency EOY Grade K," "Nonsense Word Fluency EOY Grade 1," "Oral Reading Fluency 2.1 Grade 1," "Oral Reading Fluency 3.1 Grade 3," "Maze BOY Grade 5," "Spelling BOY Grade 2," "RAN Objects Form 1," and "Benchmark Overview Report Delight Valley" graphic courtesy of Acadience Learning, Acadiencelearning.org. Copyright © by Acadience Learning LLC; 64, 68: "Letter Naming Fluency" and "Word Reading Fluency" forms from the 8th Edition of Dynamic Indicators of Basic Early Literacy Skills (DIBELS®). Copyright © 2023 by University of Oregon. Reprinted by permission; 84: "Form A Student Scoring Form: Phonics Screener for Intervention™ (PSI™)" from the 95 Phonics Screener for Intervention™ (PSI). Used with permission from 95 Percent Group, LLC; "UFLI Foundations Intervention Placement Test" by Holly B. Lane. Copyright © 2025 by University of Florida Literacy Institute. Reprinted by permission; 86: "Prosody Assessment Rating Scale" page 334 from *Teaching Reading Sourcebook, 3rd Edition*, 2018 by Arena Press. Copyright © by CORE, Inc. Reprinted by permission of Consortium on Reaching Excellence In Education, Inc.; 123–125: "Elements of Direct, Explicit Instruction" chart from *Explicit Instruction: Elective and Efficient Teaching* by Anita L. Archer and Charles A. Hughes. Copyright © 2011 by The Guilford Press. Reprinted by permission of Guilford Publications, Inc. All rights reserved.

ISBN 979-8-225-01170-3

2 3 4 5 6 7 8 9 10 40 34 33 32 31 30 29 28 27 26

Scholastic Inc., 557 Broadway, New York, NY 10012

Contents

Acknowledgments

To our husbands, Marty McGrory and Gerard Winn, whose steady encouragement carried us through every chapter, and our children, Matthew McGrory, James McGrory, Olivia Winn, and Eva Winn, who so generously support the time our work takes us away from home—all in service of helping every student learn to read.

To Pam Kastner, for crafting such a thoughtful and generous foreword, and to our early reviewers—Lindsay Kemeny, Una Malcolm, Kelly Powell-Smith, Amy Siracusano, and Kim Wright—this book is better because of you. Special thanks as well to Katy Woods for her contributions.

We are grateful to the many colleagues and friends who supported us in this project, including Matt Burns, Elsa Cárdenas-Hagan, Tiffany Hogan, Susan Brady, Katharine Beals, and Sonia Cabell. Your insights, encouragement, and conversations shaped our thinking.

With deep appreciation to Roland Good and Ruth Kaminski for their research and leadership in the field, which has inspired so much of our work.

To our Scholastic team—our supportive editor and cheerleader, Ray Coutu, along with Sarah Longhi and Tara Welty—thank you for believing in this project and guiding it with care.

Finally, our gratitude to the behind-the-scenes teams at Scholastic in design, production, author support, and marketing. Your expertise and dedication brought this book to life.

Foreword by Pam Kastner

I entered teaching as a kindergarten teacher full of conviction. I was certain that if I surrounded children with books, modeled a love of reading, and encouraged them to discover stories, they would become readers. I was a staunch believer in balanced literacy and whole language, and for a time, I thought it was enough. The read-alouds were joyful, the classroom buzzed with activity, and children seemed engaged.

But then came the students who didn't thrive, despite my print-rich classroom, the many leveled books I provided, or the encouragement I offered. Their slow progress and frustration haunted me. I didn't know what to do because my framework had no answers for them.

It was assessment that saved me. I moved beyond running records and observation tools to real, evidence-based assessment: universal screening, diagnostic assessment, progress monitoring, and outcome assessment. Evidence-based assessment showed me what I had been missing. It revealed not just what children couldn't yet do, but what they needed next. It was the compass that provided direction and the catalyst that led me to gaining the knowledge and instructional practices my students deserved.

That discovery reshaped my teaching forever. Assessment was not the end of instruction, a way to summarize what my students had learned—it was the beginning. It gave me the tools to see individual children more clearly, to meet them where they were, and to move them forward. It gave me what every teacher longs for: the ability to help every child learn to read.

That is the heartbeat of *Reading Assessment Done Right*.

In education, assessment has too often been seen as a foe—something to dread, an obligation that takes time away from teaching. This book asks us to imagine something different: assessment as a friend. A guide that helps us notice, question, and most importantly, act. A tool that prevents failure instead of documenting it after the fact.

Stephanie and Kate bring unique strengths to this work. Kate, as a practicing classroom teacher, shows how these ideas live and breathe in real classrooms with real students. Stephanie, a national leader in assessment and Multi-Tiered Systems of Support (MTSS), distills decades of research and practice into a roadmap schools can follow. Together, they make the case for assessment not as a burden, but as the very mechanism by which we can deliver on the promise of literacy for all.

The questions this book raises are immediate and instructional: What does this student's progress tell me about my next steps? How do I refine my teaching so every child advances? By asking yourself questions like those, you'll begin your journey and possibly have a ripple effect outward to inspire colleagues and systems to change. For leaders, the questions are broader: What story is our data telling us about the whole system? How do we build structures that sustain effective practice across classrooms? With the explicit tools and processes provided in this book, teachers and leaders can transform scattered practices into cohesive systems, always remembering that data is more than numbers. It represents the names and lives of each child in the school system who deserves the right to read.

We assess not just to measure, but to empower.

The brilliance of *Reading Assessment Done Right* lies not only in its technical precision but also in its insistence that prevention is possible, and that assessment is a lever by which we can achieve that goal. The result is not another book that describes assessment in the abstract, but in the concrete. It is a road map that insists on action—action that can be taken today, in your classroom. The accessible structure and wealth of practical examples enable you to apply Stephanie and Kate's tools and techniques for evidence-based improvement.

Reading is more than a skill. It is the great equalizer, the civil right of our time. To equip teachers and leaders with the knowledge of how assessment informs instruction and intervention, as this book does, is to ensure access, freedom, and opportunity for all children.

That is why this book matters so deeply. It is not simply about assessment. It is about children—their futures, their dignity, and their right to the power of literacy.

May this book not only inform you but also inspire you. May it give you the tools and the courage to act. And may it remind us all that assessment, done right, is about changing lives.

Pam Kastner, Ed.D., Literacy Consultant; Contributing Faculty Member, Mount Saint Joseph University's Reading Science Doctoral Program; President of The Reading League, Pennsylvania

Introduction by Kate Winn

It was an assessment that first sent me down the science-of-reading rabbit hole. Picture it: Downeyville, 2016. (Any *Golden Girls* fans out there?) While I had been teaching for 16 years, it was my first year in kindergarten. I sat down with little Stuart, opened up the very first book in the leveled assessment kit, and waited for the magic to happen.

The students had been participating in isolated "letter of the week" lessons for months, doing "sight word" flash cards, and even taking home little readers that contained patterned text and picture cues to build their confidence as they pointed to and guessed the words. Surely Stuart was ready to go on the scoreboard at Level 1 by now!

Alas, he was not. Dismayed, I looked on as he turned page after page, glancing first at each picture and then proceeding to guess at the words—not just the words that were not yet "decodable" (a term I was not familiar with then) and would require Stuart to make guesses based on the pictures, but he also missed the sight words we had practiced as well as words made up of sounds from phonics lessons that I had taught.

Flip. *Oooh, this page includes* "truck." *He should get that one!*

Picture glance and... "dump truck."

Okay, well, there are a lot of letters in that one, and /t/ *and* /d/ *are similar* (voiced and unvoiced sounds were also not yet in my repertoire).

Flip. *Yes—*"bus"*! He has to get this one!*

Picture glance and... "school bus."

Nope, not even at Level 1 yet... but what could I do about it? And then the light bulb went on. Not only was my instruction clearly not effective, but this assessment was not actually giving me any information that I could use to teach Stuart (or any of my students) to read. What was happening?

In my eight years previously teaching second, third, and fourth grades, I had loved sitting down with students on testing days. I mean, sure, it took hours out of the week, but the rest of the students were good to read silently or engage in freewriting while I completed assessments.

Assessment has been the biggest game changer for me... and over the last few years I have proclaimed that to all who would listen.

While my number-one happy place at school is in the rocking chair, reading a rich picture book to my captive audience at the carpet, listening to students read is a close second. I got excited when a child moved up a reading level or two, approaching the level I thought she was supposed to hit by the end of that grade—a level I now know is arbitrary.

But what about students who weren't moving up? At that time, I was just told to keep doing what I was doing, and hopefully the silent reading time, literature circles, reading passage worksheets, and inconsistent word work lessons would do the trick to help them "improve"—whatever that meant. I didn't even know enough to wonder which knowledge or skills (like phonemic awareness, specific phonics patterns, or strategies for reading multisyllabic words) could help them improve. But now in kindergarten, I was responsible for teaching students to read from scratch—and I was not prepared for it.

Back to little Stuart. I thanked him, sent him back to playtime, and firmly resolved to do better. My deep dive into the science of reading followed, and I would say "the rest is history," only here we are right now in the present with so much more work to do.

Why Stephanie and I Wrote This Book

Assessment has been the biggest game changer for me in terms of literacy instruction, and over the last few years I have proclaimed that to all who would listen, on my podcast, in webinars, and on social media.

As I devoured every book I could find on the science of reading, one day the thought hit me: Frontline teachers desperately need a book about reading assessment because it's a lot—screening and diagnostics and progress monitoring, oh my!

I knew I could bring the educator perspective (and so much new learning) to a book, but I also had the perfect person in mind to write it with me. Already an avid follower of Stephanie Stollar after joining her online Reading Science Academy, I realized that either we would need to write this book together, or I would be citing "Stollar" on every page, which might look a bit silly!

While it took me a while to get up the nerve to ask her, Stephanie enthusiastically jumped on board, and unsurprisingly had the same idea of a book to bring research and evidence-based reading assessment practices to classroom teachers everywhere.

Stephanie also assured me that I wasn't the only teacher with questions about reading assessments, because over the years she has heard similar concerns to mine from many educators:

- "Reading is so complex—I don't know how to get to the bottom of what's going on with my students."
- "I don't have enough time for all of these reading assessments and I don't understand their purpose."
- "My district requires me to use assessments that don't answer my questions, but I don't know where to begin to advocate for better tools."
- "At team meetings I just smile and nod when other educators and professionals share test scores that I don't understand, as I'm too embarrassed to speak up."
- "I have data, but no idea what to do with it."
- "It's so hard to meet the reading needs of all my students as the only adult in the classroom."

With Stephanie's broad expertise and extensive system-level knowledge and experience, along with my practical classroom applications, we are thrilled to bring *Reading Assessment Done Right* to you, responding to the above concerns and more, so you can be efficient, effective, and confident with your reading assessment practices, leading to success for all of your students!

How This Book Is Organized

The book is organized into three parts to give you what you need to understand and implement various types of reading assessments.

The first part, Chapters 1 to 3, gives you the background you need to dive into reading assessment, including essential skill areas to assess, the fundamentals of assessment you may not have learned in college, why we need to de-implement some of our traditional assessments, and the big pictures of Multi-Tiered Systems of Support (MTSS) and the Collaborative Improvement Cycle (CIC).

The second part, Chapters 4 to 7, dives into all the burning "need to know" information about the four types of assessments:

- Universal Screening
- Diagnostic Assessment
- Progress Monitoring
- Outcome Assessment

With key questions, characteristics, tips, and examples for all four categories, plus anecdotes and pitfalls from our own experiences, we want to set you up for success with reading assessment within your classroom.

The third part, Chapter 8, empowers you to use reading assessment data to inform your classroom instruction. It contains case studies, advice on determining instructional targets, tips for grouping, considerations for intensifying instruction as necessary, and more.

Let's get started!

Reading Assessment: Friend, Not Foe

CHAPTER 1

Reading instruction is in transition. Educators, parents/guardians, and legislators are demanding change. It is well understood that we are failing in our most basic obligation to teach reading, especially to our most vulnerable students (National Center for Education Statistics, 2024). But what are we going to do about it? More measurement of the problem isn't likely to help. For decades, teachers have been handed mandated reading assessments and held accountable for results, and yet, student outcomes haven't improved. How can that contradiction be resolved? Have we been measuring the wrong things, in the wrong ways? It's time to answer those essential questions. It's time to change reading assessment from a foe that is dreaded and feared to an irreplaceable friend.

We believe in the power of assessment to improve reading outcomes. We have lived it!

We believe in the power of assessment to improve reading outcomes. We have lived it!

Kate is a more effective reading teacher as a result of having the right data and using it to take action. Stephanie has experienced school-wide transformation by leading teams to design and implement systems that empower every teacher to use assessments as effectively as Kate. Our goal in writing this book is to empower you with knowledge and tools for using assessment to improve reading outcomes for all your students.

The science-of-reading movement is fueled by teachers like you who recognize the gap between what is possible and the reality of abysmal reading achievement test results. How can we be failing so many students?

At the heart of the science of reading are four fundamental understandings that inform the way we think about reading assessment:

1. Reading comprehension is the product of word recognition and language comprehension.
2. Most reading problems are preventable.
3. Learning occurs when our students store new information in long-term memory.
4. The reading problem can't be solved one student at a time.

In this chapter, we explore the relationship between those understandings and the decisions you make about selecting and using assessments.

Reading Comprehension Is the Goal—and We Can Measure It

In 1986, Gough and Tunmer proposed a theory called the Simple View of Reading (SVR), claiming that only two capacities are necessary for reading comprehension: word recognition and language comprehension. They depicted the SVR as a multiplication problem to stress that each capacity is necessary (when you multiply anything by zero you get zero), and neither is sufficient on its own for reading comprehension. Hundreds of studies over several decades confirm that the SVR is true for all students, including multilingual learners and students with disabilities, which is why it's often included in professional development on the science of reading.

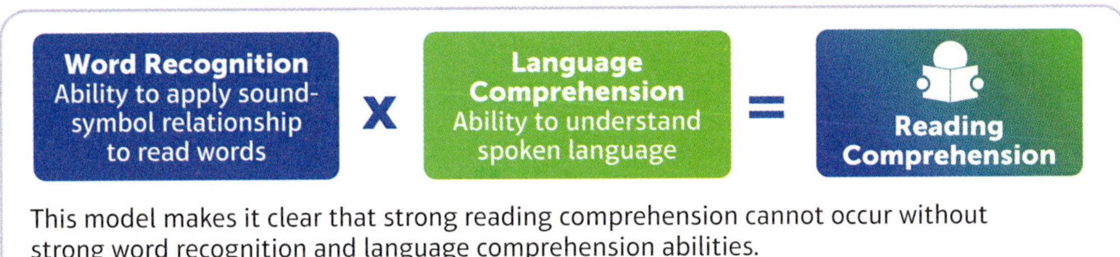

This model makes it clear that strong reading comprehension cannot occur without strong word recognition and language comprehension abilities.

(Gough & Tunmer, 1986)

Within the SVR domains are several skills that are essential for proficient reading:

- **Word-recognition skills** are essential building blocks for cracking the written English code. Hoover and Tunmer (2021) define word recognition as the ability to effortlessly recognize words to gain access to the meaning of words during reading. Accurate and efficient word reading starts with an awareness of phonemes, the smallest units of spoken words. Students must also learn to connect phonemes to sound spellings, or graphemes, to encode and decode words, which is a much more challenging task. Knowledge of morphemes, or meaningful parts of words, aids in reading and spelling.

- **Language-comprehension skills** must be built along with word recognition because literacy is based in oral language. Language comprehension is the ability to gain meaning from speech (Hoover & Tunmer, 2021). Vocabulary breadth and depth are essential aspects of the language comprehension that supports reading comprehension (Stahl & Nagy, 2006). When a student's vocabulary is broad, he or she knows a little bit about a lot of words (e.g., "I've heard the word *livid* before and I know it's not good, but I don't know exactly what it means"). A deep vocabulary involves knowing a lot about specific words to the point of confidently and accurately using them in his or her own speech or writing (e.g., "Mom was livid when she saw how messy my room was"—a direct quote from one of Kate's daughters!). Knowing word meanings is not enough. Students must also know what words mean in various contexts. They must know English syntax, for example, to understand who was doing the chasing in this sentence: "The girl the dog chased ran into the house." Understanding what you read depends on understanding spoken language, or listening comprehension.
- **Reading comprehension**, the ability to gain meaning from print (Hoover & Tunmer, 2021), is complex. It relates to listening comprehension in that they both involve gaining and making meaning, and differs in that listening comprehension involves making meaning from spoken words and reading comprehension requires making meaning from printed words.

Essential Skill Areas to Measure

We can use the Simple View of Reading to help us focus on what to assess and what to teach. When students acquire both word-recognition and language-comprehension skills, they are far more likely to comprehend what they read. Within word recognition and language comprehension are five essential skill areas that every student must develop to become a proficient reader:

- phonemic awareness
- the alphabetic principle and basic phonics
- vocabulary and oral language
- text-reading fluency
- reading comprehension

The target skills in those areas are not nice-to-haves; they are must-haves for every student. Research tells us that students who have them are on their way to being readers, and students who don't have them are likely to struggle with reading unless they get help (National Institute of Child Health and Human Development, 2000; Castles et al., 2018). Therefore, the five skills are excellent assessment and teaching targets, particularly for multilingual learners, students living in poverty, and students with disabilities. If we know early in any grade that a student needs support in one or more of those skills, and we teach them to grade-level goals—BAM!—the student goes from at risk to on track!

Essential Skill Area	Description	Example
Phonemic Awareness	Knowledge of the sound structure of spoken language at the level of individual phonemes	Say the sounds in the word *cat.* /c/ /a/ /t/
The Alphabetic Principle and Basic Phonics	Using the understanding that letters represent spoken sounds in order to decode and spell	Spell the word *cat.* Read the word *cat.*
Vocabulary and Oral Language	Word knowledge	What does the word *cat* mean?
Text-Reading Fluency	Accurate and automatic text reading	Reading a passage accurately and automatically enough to understand the content
Reading Comprehension	Gaining and making meaning from print	Understanding what is read

What does all that mean for assessment? It means some things are absolutely essential to assess. Most educators agree that too much instructional time is spent on assessment, and we don't want to make more work for you. In fact, we want to help you assess more efficiently! Because converging research has determined the essential skill areas, they should be prioritized for assessment and instruction. Equipping students with those skills will make the difference between becoming skilled readers or struggling readers. Note that while we describe these skills separately, and they are often assessed in isolation, it is important to integrate them in instruction.

We Can Prevent Reading Problems

Did you know that most reading problems can be prevented by assessing and teaching within essential skill areas in the early grades (Torgesen, 2002)? Even before students are reading continuous text, their performance on essential skills predicts end-of-first-grade reading. Students' reading performance at the end of first grade predicts their reading performance at the end of fourth grade and beyond (Francis et al., 1996; Juel, 1988; Torgesen & Burgess, 1998). As such, we can know which students are likely to struggle as early as preK, giving us lots of time to reverse that prediction and prevent a reading problem from happening in the first place—a key driver of Kate's teaching. While prevention in K and early grade 1 is best, intervention early in any grade is helpful (Good et al., 2012).

What does that mean for assessment? It means we have to prevent reading problems, as well as find and fix reading difficulties as early as possible. It means ending practices such as grade retention, delaying the start of kindergarten, giving students "the gift of time," and taking a wait-and-see approach. As you will learn in Chapters 4 and 6, universal-screening and progress-monitoring assessments are powerful tools for prevention and early intervention that guard against a "wait-to-fail" approach.

We Can—and Must—Ensure Students Learn It

Learning to read is bound by the same constraints as all human learning. We have the capacity to pay attention to a limited amount of information at any given moment. Cognitive scientists call this *short-term memory*, or *working memory*. Working memory has limited capacity. The goal of teaching is moving information from short-term into long-term memory, which has unlimited storage capacity. What we think of as "learning" is simply storage in long-term memory.

The instructional hierarchy outlines three phases of learning (Burns et al., 2010; Haring et al., 1978; VanDerHeyden & Burns, 2023), which proceed from the *acquisition* phase, where responses are slow, effortful, and include many errors; to the *fluency-building* phase, where responses are accurate and effortless; and ultimately to the *generalization and adaptation* phase, where reading can be used to acquire new information and build knowledge. Learning increases when instruction is matched to the phase of the instructional hierarchy the learner is in.

Learn more about accuracy and fluency from Stephanie here.

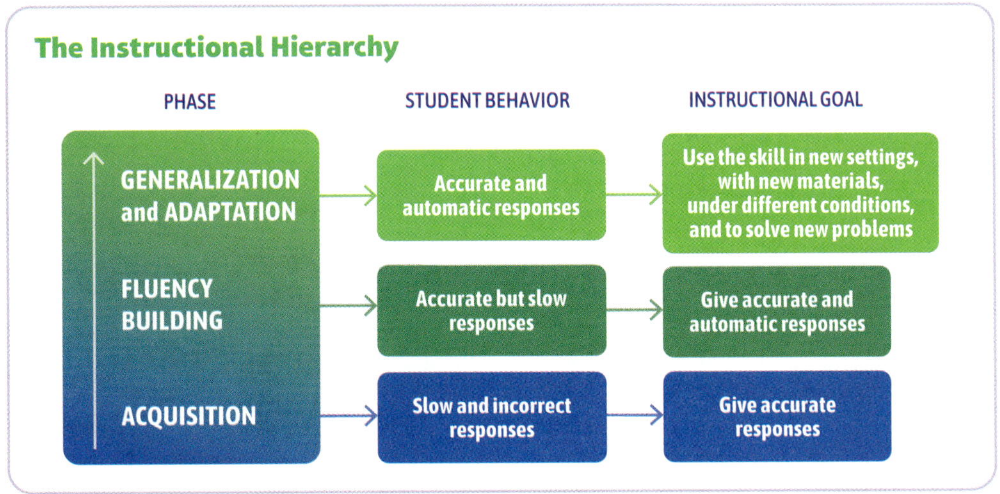

What does that mean for assessment? It means to measure automaticity and not just accuracy. This is easily done by measuring rate or correct items (such as phonemes, letter sounds, or words) per minute. Timed assessments of the essential skills are useful indicators of whether students have learned the building blocks of literacy at a level of automaticity, which reflects storage in long-term memory. It also means those of us who are aware of the instructional hierarchy can target our instruction to where students are on the hierarchy. As we explain in Chapter 5, we can be more effective when we have data on where students are in the instructional hierarchy and focus instruction accordingly—practices that are particularly important for multilingual learners and students with disabilities.

We Can't Solve the Nation's Reading Crisis One Student at a Time

Because, according to the *National Assessment of Educational Progress* (National Center for Education Statistics, 2024), more than half of all U.S. students are not proficient readers. Your school is likely to be filled with struggling and at-risk readers, some of whom are probably in your own classroom! And yet, local policies tend to focus solely on finding low-performing students and giving them reading interventions. That approach would be fine if there weren't so many low-performing students! Trying to solve this problem one student at a time is exhausting many teachers and school leaders. Who wants to plan and deliver instruction for multiple small groups with multiple needs? Not us!

We can step back from attempting to intervene with students one by one and instead attend to the instructional systems or conditions in which each student is learning to read, taking into account schedule, materials, educator knowledge, grouping formats, and teams working together for reading improvement. In our experience, the biggest impact on all students, especially multilingual learners and students with disabilities, comes from analyzing the way schools are organized to get things done and evaluating the aspects of those systems that are supporting teaching and learning and improving the ones that aren't.

That systemic approach is called Multi-Tiered System of Supports (MTSS). As you will learn in Chapter 3, the MTSS model of reading improvement involves teams working together at all levels of the educational system (district/board, school, grade, and student).

Burning Question

Are timed assessments necessary and, if so, do they cause anxiety?

We've heard this concern relating to literacy and math assessments. So, on her podcast *Reading Road Trip* (2024), Kate asked researcher and policy adviser Amanda VanDerHeyden for her expert opinion.

The Importance of Timed Assessments
"You cannot build fluency without having timed practice and timed assessments. You could have two kids, both of whom are 100 percent accurate, one who can only read two words correctly in one minute and one who can read 130 words correctly in one minute. The kid who can read 130 is way more proficient. But they both have 100 percent accuracy. Accuracy runs out of steam. When it hits 100 percent, it's got a ceiling. So the way you distinguish the proficiency of those two kids is to give them the same amount of time."

Timed Assessments and Anxiety
"Avoidance of the stimulus that is arousing your anxiety can become a way to limit your life space and your adaptive opportunity in the world.... It's beginning to look like the first onset of anxiety actually comes after weak skill proficiency. So, weak skill proficiency precedes the onset of anxiety, and then it's a bidirectional feed."

"That matters because, as teachers... one of the ways you can prevent academic anxiety in your students is to build skill proficiency and make correct responding easier. It's actually one of the reasons we don't want to use productive struggle and inquiry-based learning in the acquisition phase of learning. We are inviting anxiety when we do that."

While we, as educators, know the value of timed assessments, we can ease student anxiety by presenting them in a low-stakes way, for example by not displaying results publicly or connecting them to class rewards systems, etc., where there is a potential for a student to be embarrassed.

Connecting Assessment to Instruction

The great news is that the five essential skill areas we described earlier in this chapter can be taught! When they are taught directly and explicitly, students learn them, which greatly increases their chances of becoming skilled readers.

In the MTSS model, assessments of the five essential literacy skills cover four purposes:

1. **Screening:** Brief indicators that tell us which students and systems are at risk
2. **Diagnostic:** In-depth assessment to inform next steps for instruction
3. **Progress monitoring:** Alternate forms of screening measures to indicate the need to change instruction or keep it as is
4. **Outcome:** Looking back to see if instruction worked

That said, some reading assessments aren't as useful for instruction, such as computer-adaptive, universal screening assessments that are designed to determine if groups of students are on track, but don't tell us what students need to learn. Other assessments don't measure things that improve reading when they are taught, such as auditory processing and rapid automatized naming. Why bother taking time away from teaching to give these if they don't inform instruction? And lastly, there are assessments that measure things, such as motivation and interest, which are more of an outcome rather than a cause of skilled reading. Those assessments aren't worth your time because you can just as easily gather that information through observation and interviews.

Curriculum-Based Measures

We prefer reading assessments that directly link to instruction because they tell us what our students know and need to learn next. Low on the alphabetic principle? Teach phonics. Low on text-reading fluency? Build fluency in text. Low on vocabulary? Teach the meanings of words. The category of assessment that links to instruction is Curriculum-Based Measures (CBM). CBMs are brief (usually one minute) indicators of the essential literacy skills that can be used for universal screening and progress monitoring. They are global indicators of risk and growth, not tests of previously taught content. Examples of CBMs include Acadience Reading (Good et al., 2020), Dynamic Indicators of Basic Early Literacy Skills (DIBELS®) 8th Edition (University of Oregon, 2021), aimswebPlus (NCS Pearson, 2018), and FastBridge CBMreading (FastBridge Learning, 2019). CBMs were originally designed for progress monitoring, have been expanded to use for universal screening, and are ideal for use in data-based decision-making. More information on the use of CBMs is included throughout the book.

Avoiding Testing Pitfalls

Obviously, we are big fans of reading assessment. That said, we think schools spend too much time testing, which leaves less time for instruction. Keep in mind that when it comes to assessments, more is not better. We've heard of schools using as many as three different reading assessments for screening all students at the beginning, middle, and end of the year, along with writing, math, and state tests... we're tired just thinking about that! Even worse, some schools collect a lot of data but never use it. Some schools add assessments without removing ones that no longer serve teachers and students. Here's our advice: Choose only ONE assessment for each of the four categories.

Assessment Audits

To avoid pitfalls like the ones mentioned above, we recommend teacher teams do an assessment audit: an inventory of the assessments for the five essential skill areas, for each assessment purpose, used at each grade.

Go here for a blank audit template and a sample completed template.

If you keep some basic criteria in mind, you can optimize the time you spend teaching by asking the following questions before you give a test:

- Does this assessment measure something research identifies as essential?
- How much time will giving the assessment take away from instruction?
- Are there more efficient ways to get the same information?
- Will this assessment help me know what to teach tomorrow?
- Which purpose of assessment does it address?

Eight Reasons to Stop Using Traditional Assessments

We realize that the assessments we recommend in this book may be new to you, and change is hard. We also know that it's easier to take on new things if something old and ineffective is de-implemented.

In this section, we share a big menu item you can slide off your plate immediately: many reading assessments that we teachers have used historically! The assessments we've often used in the past, in which we listen to students read an entire leveled passage, untimed, and note the number and type of errors, are usually referred to as Informal Reading Inventories (IRIs), or running records. Here are some reasons you can safely retire those assessments.

1. They don't mean what we thought they did.

Kate used to get excited when she completed a running record and saw a student jump a few levels ("Wow—she's gone from Level K to Level O!") until she heard Matt Burns (Burns et al., 2015) share that the difference between assumed difficulty levels is not equal. What does that mean? The difference between Levels A and B is not necessarily the same as the difference between Levels B and C. Also, there is a lot of subjectivity involved with assigning students to levels of text. A student scoring at Level O might actually have the same reading skills as a student who scored anywhere from Levels M to Q!

Like many teachers, Kate also thought that having students answer text-specific questions was the best indicator we had of reading comprehension, which is not the case. Just wait until you get to Chapter 4 and find out what the best indicator actually is. If you're like Kate, it will blow your mind!

2. They don't help us plan next steps for instruction.

As we'll be talking about later, it's important to form small groups based on targeted foundational skills, not on arbitrary lettered or numbered levels, and traditional assessments don't tell us what foundational skills each student has or doesn't have. Kate discovered one of the most frustrating things about assessing reading—she might know a child who was at reading Level 12 and was supposed to be at Level 19, but what was the difference? What was she supposed to teach next? Vowel teams? Multisyllabic words? Now Kate uses targeted assessments that help her form flexible groups based on very specific needs. That also means she avoids locking students into the same group for long periods (once a Bluebird, always a Bluebird) and instead can move them in and out of groups as necessary, based on results of progress monitoring.

The chart on the next page, based on data shared with Matt Burns by a classroom teacher, shows 16 students who all came out at Level G in a running record. That should mean they're all around the same skill level, right? But wait: Look at the huge range in terms of their accuracy percentages and words correct per minute (WCPM) scores on an Oral Reading Fluency assessment, which you'll learn more about in Chapter 4. Clearly these students do not have the same instructional needs.

3. They don't accurately predict reading risk.

It's a misconception that running records and IRIs can accurately predict reading risk. In one study, a popular running record system was found to be accurate at identifying at-risk readers only about 50 percent of the time, when compared to a universal screener (Burns & Parker, 2014). As Burns and Parker write in *Curriculum-Based Assessment for Instructional Design*, "If you wanted to use [running record] data to identify students as needing additional support, you could spend thousands of dollars to purchase the materials, spend hours to train the teachers how to administer the test, dedicate hundreds of hours of instructional time to conducting the assessments, or you could invest 25 cents; simply take a quarter and flip it every time a student enters the door and you will get it right nearly as often."

Running Record Level	ORF WCPM	ORF Accuracy
G	30	77%
G	37	88%
G	30	94%
G	32	87%
G	58	89%
G	80	98%
G	26	93%
G	27	84%
G	36	86%
G	30	77%
G	31	82%
G	44	90%
G	47	90%
G	61	95%
G	70	100%
G	17	77%

4. They're not cost- or time-efficient.

While the financial cost may not be coming out of our pockets, the time cost to students and teachers hits us harder! What are all of the other students doing while you are assessing each student? While the time and money might be worth it to get instructionally useful data, most traditional assessments just don't give us that, plus many of the assessment tools we recommend in upcoming chapters are available free of charge.

5. They don't all actually assess reading.

The earliest levels (with predictable/patterned books) aren't in fact assessing reading, as students are not expected to decode, but instead to look at the pictures and repeat the patterns to come up with (often guessing) the words in the text. The "three-cueing" practice (also known as MSV, where students are encouraged to use meaning, syntax, and visual cues to determine the words instead of focusing on letter-sound correspondences) runs contrary to the research on how students first learn to read (Ehri, 2020).

6. They don't meet the scientific criteria necessary to be strong assessments.

Traditional assessments don't meet all of the scientific criteria we're looking for in assessment. Some claim to, but don't produce the evidence. According to Burns and Parker (2014), most IRIs do not report their reliability data, and "assessment tools without reported reliability are the equivalent of a Ouija board; the information they reveal may be accurate, but we have no way of knowing for sure." If you're of a certain age, you probably remember the Wendy's commercial in which a feisty, gray-haired woman asked, "Where's the beef?" of a competitor's hamburger. We ask, "Where's the proof?" of traditional assessments!

7. They don't assess automaticity.

We've always looked at student accuracy when reading, which is essential. However, traditional assessments typically do not include a measure of automaticity or rate, which is a must-have when determining a student's skill level. You'll learn more about that in Chapter 4.

8. They don't help us find good texts for students to read.

When teaching upper elementary grades, Kate would use a child's "level," as determined by a running record, to select books for that child to read independently in class, until she learned how ineffective that was. In one study, researchers had students read books at their assigned "level" (e.g., Level L) and used an Oral Reading Fluency assessment to categorize each student as a high, low, or average reader (Burns et al., 2015). Results showed that the leveled assessment underestimated the average and high readers; books at their "level" were too easy for them. On the other hand, it overestimated the weak readers, with 58 percent of them scoring at the frustration level in terms of their accuracy percentage while reading those books. These were definitely not "just right" books for all the students!

To sum it up, traditional assessments do not meet the purposes of assessment as we see them. If we can't use data the assessments provide for screening, diagnosing, progress monitoring, and outcome evaluation—or for planning instruction throughout the process—why do it?

Burning Question

What should I do with all my leveled books?

Although you may not be using leveled books for assessments or guided reading, you can still put them to good use. For example, you can repurpose them as material for classroom libraries and organize nonfiction books by topic to support content-area instructions.

This shift in mindset may seem like a big hurdle for you. But by the time you finish this book, we hope you'll feel empowered to not only use evidence-based assessment practices but also to articulate the rationale to colleagues and parents/guardians.

Burning Question

What if my administrator is still requiring traditional assessments?

We know not all districts are like Kate's, where principals were asked to return running record kits to the board office on a professional development day in exchange for coffee and donuts. From there, the kits were disassembled, with components repurposed or recycled where possible.

In some districts and schools, teachers are still required to use a running record or IRI as a reading assessment. If you're in one of those districts or schools, what can you do? Of course, we recommend you comply with mandates. However, we also recommend that you get the information you need to improve reading outcomes for your students as quickly as possible. We've seen teachers do both for a short time period: Continue to give the required assessments, while adding in a more direct measure of the essential skill areas for a few or even all of their students. Stephanie has worked with teachers who have done this and then shared the data with their school leaders. They've been able to show that not only can they get the same information about who needs help, but they can also target their instruction, group students, and monitor progress in less time.

We also encourage you to share this chapter and the resources mentioned in it with your coworkers and school leaders. There is strength in numbers! District and school administrators are more likely to pay attention when teachers come to them as a united front.

In Closing, Remember...

When you rely on the Simple View of Reading and the five essential skill areas to guide assessment selection, you will measure the skills research shows are necessary for proficient reading. The MTSS model and the instructional hierarchy provide additional guidance for efficient assessment that maximizes the possibility of effective instruction with a focus on prevention and early intervention. You can make room for adopting instructionally relevant assessments by de-implementing those that don't give you the information you need about your students. The rest of the book will support you to take action on these big ideas with tools and processes for getting results for all students. Coming up next in Chapter 2, we discuss and clarify seven fundamentals of reading assessment that every teacher should be familiar with.

CHAPTER 2

The Nuts and Bolts of Reading Assessment

Teachers aren't always prepared with information that can help guide their work. For example, Kate learned nothing about reading assessment in college, and it's possible you didn't either! And let's face it, the topic of assessment can be confusing and intimidating, so gaining knowledge about it on our own might seem overwhelming.

We won't lie: There are many scientific terms in this chapter, and it may seem like a lot. At the same time, we know how busy you are, so we present those terms as clearly and succinctly as possible. We promise that the rest of the book is full of the practical ways to apply assessment essentials in your classroom, but we also want to make sure that you, as a frontline educator, have access to essential learning. We want you to feel confident when your school's speech-language pathologist or school psychologist shows you a report on one of your students, or when a parent or guardian shares the results of an outside evaluation. After all, you are an important member of teams making decisions about students.

Seven Assessment Fundamentals

In this chapter, by focusing on the nuts and bolts of reading assessment, or seven fundamentals, we aim to inform and empower you in three ways:

- To give you information to make good choices about which assessments to use
- To show you how to use assessments in the ways they are constructed and for the purposes for which they are designed
- To help you understand the results of those assessments

We also want you to understand the tests given by other education professionals so you can be a full participant in team conversations about the reading performance of your students. We cover topics such as formal and informal assessments, validity, reliability, standardization, types of scores, and interpretation of scores. This guidance aligns with testing standards from professional associations such as the National Council of Teachers of English (NCTE, 2009) and the AERA Standards for Educational and Psychological Testing (Joint Committee on Standards for Educational and Psychological Testing, 2014). We refer you to those associations for more detailed information.

1. Ways of Knowing

There are so many ways to gather information about your students, ranging from informal hunches and gut feelings to formal assessment methods. Formal assessments are important when the results are used to make key decisions, such as who needs help (universal screening), what help is needed (diagnostic assessment), and if the help is working (progress monitoring).

Let's say you have a sore throat. Based on your experience with and intuition about sore throats—and the fact that your schedule allows you to stay home for the next few days—you might not need to know if your illness is due to spring allergies or strep throat. But if you need to get on an airplane or go to work tomorrow, you might seek a formal assessment to determine what's causing the sore throat so you know what action to take—leave home or not.

The same thing goes for teaching. The importance of the decision determines how formal the information gathering needs to be and, therefore, which assessment to select. When making important teaching decisions, such as when you're teaching beginning and struggling readers, it is important to base your instructional moves on complete and accurate information.

What Data Should I Use to Decide Who Needs Help?

We teachers collect thousands of data points about our students each day, some formal and some informal. If you observe a student struggling to sound out a word, you might think about what you learned about decoding in a professional development workshop you had last week, or you might recall your experience last year with a student who had dyslexia. If the student's struggle is a one-time occurrence, you might file it away for future reference. But if you observe a pattern of similar struggles, and the student received intervention last year and has siblings with dyslexia, you might escalate to more formal data collection.

Pay attention when you notice things in the classroom that trigger concerns. However, keep in mind, information that you collect under controlled conditions is more trustworthy when you need to make important decisions. You can be confident about that information as opposed to information based on hunches, secondhand reports, observations, and recall of past experiences. As Jan Hasbrouck warns (2024), "Although observation of student performance is essential to inform our instructional decisions, professional educators must not rely simply on 'cardiac assessment,' that is, 'in my heart I know what is right for my students.'"

This graphic shows how confidently we can approach our decisions based on the type of data we're using. Keep in mind that it's only when we've combined our observations and experiences with students along with direct measurements of their essential literacy skills that we can make logical, confident choices about next steps for instruction. We will help you learn to do that in later chapters!

Level of Confidence	Form of Data Collection
HIGH ↑ ↓ LOW	• formal testing • informal testing • observation • self-report, survey, interview • advice from a trusted source • recall • intuition

2. Testing Basics

The Knowledge and Practice Standards from the International Dyslexia Association (2018) are the gold standard for teacher preparation and professional development. Standard 3 addresses what teachers need to know about assessment, including understanding the purposes of assessment, using Curriculum-Based Measures, understanding reliability and validity, interpreting the test results from other educators, and sharing assessment results with parents and guardians. All of those topics are addressed in this book.

Standard 5 addresses professional dispositions and practices, including respecting confidentiality. Best practice and ethical guidelines tell us that assessment results should be shared only with other educators who have a professional reason to know the information to help the student. Test reports and scoring forms can be housed in a student's confidential cumulative folder and sent on to the next teacher or school. Otherwise, how a student scored on a test is no one's business but yours (and their parents' and guardians').

Some forms of formal testing, such as special education evaluations, require signed parent permission. Even if you are doing informal assessment to fine-tune your teaching and don't need parent permission, it is important to inform and engage caregivers at the earliest sign of difficulty. When you are engaging the support of other educators, such as reading specialists, school psychologists, or speech-language pathologists, or when you are providing supplemental intervention to a student, make sure parents and guardians are aware of your concerns.

Learn more about explaining screening results to parents from Stephanie here.

Where Should You Test Students?

Try to minimize distractions by testing in a quiet location. But we get it—many schools are overcrowded, and such a location may not be an option. If you must test at the back of your room, engage the class in a quiet activity and position the student being assessed so his or her back is to the class.

Also, think creatively: In Kate's district, some teachers buddy up with a colleague to complete testing and take turns supervising both classes (on the playground, in the gym, working together in a classroom) so the other teacher can complete assessments.

To get the best possible performance from the students, make sure they are as comfortable and relaxed as possible before you begin testing them. In addition to choosing the right space, you might ask them a few innocuous questions to put them at ease. It is fine to describe the assessment in general terms, but be sure that what you tell the student focuses on gathering information to help you know how to teach them more effectively. We like the sample script provided in the *Acadience® Reading K–6 Assessment Manual* (Good & Kaminski, 2020) as a model of how to talk to students about being assessed. While Kate uses her own phrasing and doesn't provide too much detail to her kindergartners ("This helps me to know what you know, so I can help you learn more!"), they see this as a positive experience and will often cheer "Yes!" when they're called to the back table for their "one-minute activities"!

3. Validity: Measure What Matters

Validity describes the extent to which a test measures what it says it measures. Tests are not universally valid but are instead valid for the purpose for which they are designed. For example, if a test is designed to be an in-depth measure of reading achievement, it will not be a valid tool for quickly measuring growth on a daily basis. Additionally, if a test is designed to measure phonemic awareness, it will not be a valid tool for measuring reading comprehension.

Because research has converged around the five essential skill areas we outlined in Chapter 1 (phonemic awareness, phonics, vocabulary, fluency, and reading comprehension), those are the priorities to assess. It is important to select assessments of these skills that are valid, meaning studies confirm they actually measure these skills and don't just include the terms in the title of the test. The results from these tests are particularly useful because they help us prioritize instruction, without being distracted by other skills that don't contribute meaningfully to instructional decisions. The chart below lists types of validity and why they matter.

Type of Validity	Answers the Question	Why It Matters
Construct Validity	To what extent does a test measure what it says it measures?	When teachers need information about a student's skills in a particular area, they need tests that actually measure that skill.
Predictive Validity	To what extent does a score predict performance on another assessment in the future?	It is important to catch reading problems early and provide early intervention. Screening assessments should predict important future outcomes, such as how a student will perform on future reading achievement tests.
Instructional Validity (sometimes called Instructional Utility)	To what extent is a test useful for planning instruction?	Tests for diagnosing disabilities or labeling and categorizing students are not as valuable as tests that directly inform instruction.
Social Validity	To what extent do educators see value in a test?	Teachers aren't likely to use tests they don't trust.
Consequential Validity	What are the intended and unintended positive and negative social consequences of a test?	Although we can't predict all possible outcomes, we should try to predict and guard against negative consequences of testing, such as grade retention and pressure on teachers.

You'll typically see validity reported as a correlation coefficient where 1.0 is a perfect correlation between two variables. Coefficients close to 1.0 indicate:

- the test measures the construct it is designed to assess.
- the test predicts performance on another test in the future.
- the test can be used to plan instruction.

Tests with validity coefficients of at least .80 are best to use for screening decisions, and at least .90 for diagnostic decisions. Tests with validity coefficients between .30 and .60 should be used with caution, as they may not be measuring or predicting what they claim. Tests with validity coefficients less than .30 should be avoided. Social validity is the exception. Rather than being reported as a correlation coefficient, the acceptability of assessments is typically reported using surveys and rating scales. Interested in learning about the validity of a published assessment your school uses? The National Center on Intensive Intervention posts a summary of the validity of various reading assessments on its website.

Using tests with low or unknown validity, such as ones you make yourself or informal assessments downloaded from the Internet, may be okay when the stakes are low. But when making important decisions involving universal screening, diagnostic assessment, and progress monitoring, always use tests with adequate validity.

4. Reliability: Identify Skills Versus Measurement Errors

All measures of human behavior contain some amount of error. You've probably had the experience of stepping on the scale at the doctor's office and getting a slightly different result from the one you get at home. By using two different scales, error is introduced into the question about your weight. This is called *measurement error*.

Error is present in all assessments. However, when we assess reading, we should aim to minimize error and get as close as possible to a true estimate of a student's actual skills. Let's say a student scores 90 percent correct on a reading comprehension test. How many did he or she get right due to lucky guesses? How many did the student get wrong due to testing in a noisy classroom? How many did he or she answer correctly or incorrectly due to the way the test is designed? Those sources of error should be reduced, whether you're testing to determine who needs help, how many students need help, what help they need, or if the help is working.

One way to reduce measurement error is to use tests that have demonstrated *reliability*. Reliability is the extent to which an assessment gets consistent results across time, test forms, or assessors. Reliability is reported as a correlation between two variables, ranging from 0 (no relationship between the two tests) and 1.0, meaning the same score was obtained at different times, on different forms of the test, or when the test was given by different assessors. When selecting tests for universal screening and diagnostic assessment, choose tools that have reliability coefficients of at least .80, and at least .70 for progress-monitoring decisions. Tests with reliability coefficients between .40 and .70 should be used with caution, as they contain too much error for us to be confident in the results. Tests with reliability coefficients less than .40 should be avoided. The chart below lists types of reliability and why they matter.

Type of Reliability	Answers the Question	Why It Matters
Test-Retest Reliability	Is it consistent across time? We get the same results even if administered on different days.	We have more confidence in the results when they are the same across time.
Alternate Form Reliability	Is it consistent across forms of the test? We get the same results no matter which form we use.	We have more confidence in the results when they are the same across forms.
Inter-Scorer Reliability	Is it consistent across testers? We get the same results no matter who administers the test.	We have more confidence in the results when testers agree on the scores.

Test reliability and test validity are related. Unreliable tests are too inconsistent and contain too much error to be valid for any assessment purpose. A test with low reliability will not have high validity.

5. Standardization: Show What They Know

If you've ever had to drive in a raging snowstorm or speak in front of a large audience, we're sure you can relate to the way conditions impact performance, and that applies to assessments as well. Two students are likely to perform differently if one gets unlimited time and the other only gets five minutes, or if one student has the directions repeated and the other doesn't.

Maintaining the same testing conditions across students is called *standardization*. Tests should be given under standard (the same) conditions when you plan to compare students to each other or to a threshold of performance. That means using the same directions, practice items, prompts, scoring rules, and timing for all students. Standardized tests give us confidence that the scores represent what the student knows and not measurement error.

Sticking to strict standardization procedures can feel unnatural, especially if you're the kind of teacher who instinctively jumps in to support students so they respond correctly. But to give all students the same chance to show what they know, we must squelch that well-intended instinct during formal testing. When you first shift to standardized assessments, this part can be really tough ("But if I just rephrase that, he'll get it! She just needs a bit more time and I'm sure she would respond correctly!"), but it's absolutely essential to follow procedure when using standardized tests.

Select standardized tests for universal screening and progress monitoring to be sure that each time you measure a skill, you get results that reflect what the student knows. It may be less important to select standardized tests for diagnostic assessment. Some diagnostic assessments do not involve comparing students to each other, and instead involve uncovering what to teach and how to teach individual students. In Chapters 4–7, we talk about how standardization applies (and doesn't apply) to specific types of assessments.

Standardized tests require training. That training should include instruction in and practice with the standardized procedures for giving, scoring, and interpreting the test, which can usually be found in the assessment manual. One-time training is rarely enough. And because we have much more to think about than which response gets circled versus underlined, it is important to revisit assessment training periodically, and to observe each other administer assessments and offer feedback.

How Do You Make Appropriate Testing Accommodations?

Approved accommodations are exceptions to test standardization. They involve changing the testing conditions in ways the test authors allow. Students with disabilities and English learners sometimes require accommodations on tests, such as extended time, having tests read to them, or having questions read in their home language. These accommodations may be appropriate on outcome assessments, such as reading achievement tests, but they are not appropriate on the CBMs we discuss in this book because non-standardized use of these assessments means you can't compare the score to the goal.

Burning Question

How can I assess students who do not speak?

You may occasionally encounter a student who does not speak, either due to a disability or selective mutism. Because commonly used standardized assessments are not appropriate for these students, it can be difficult to determine what they know and need to learn next. We recommend trying tasks that don't require a verbal response (e.g., asking the student to gesture, point to an answer, or select among multiple-choice items), taking advantage of Augmentative and Alternative Communication (AAC) devices where possible, and seeking the support of a speech-language pathologist.

> **Burning Question**
>
> ***What is a norming sample and why is it important?***
>
> Before using a norm-referenced test, check the norming sample to be sure it represents the student(s) you will be testing. Are students in the norming sample similar to your students in terms of age, ethnicity, geographic location, English proficiency, and disability status? These variables may or may not impact the results.
>
> For example, if there were no students with dyslexia included in the norming sample, you might be cautious about interpreting the results for a student with dyslexia. On the other hand, students who are learning to read and write in English in Canada need to achieve the same level of the same skills as students in the United States, so it may not matter if Canadian students were not represented in the norms.

Publishers of CBMs, such as Acadience Reading and DIBELS 8th Edition, provide a list of approved accommodations in their assessment manuals. These include the use of a ruler or other marker for tracking, assistive listening devices, or enlarging test materials, which do not invalidate the results. Allowing extra time, repeating directions, and reading directions in a student's home language are examples of *unapproved accommodations*, which are not allowed on most standardized tests. Check with the test author or publisher before using an accommodation that is not listed as an approved accommodation in the assessment manual.

6. Raw Scores and Their Conversion

How we interpret scores is influenced by the question the test is designed to answer, its reliability and validity, and whether it requires standardized administration and scoring procedures. It's also influenced by the types of scores generated by the test. (See the chart on pages 33–35 for common types of scores.) The easiest scores to interpret are raw scores, which are simply the number of items the student got right on the test. It is best to use raw scores from screening, diagnostic, and progress-monitoring assessments because they are the easiest to understand and act on. Things get more complicated when raw scores are converted to scaled scores.

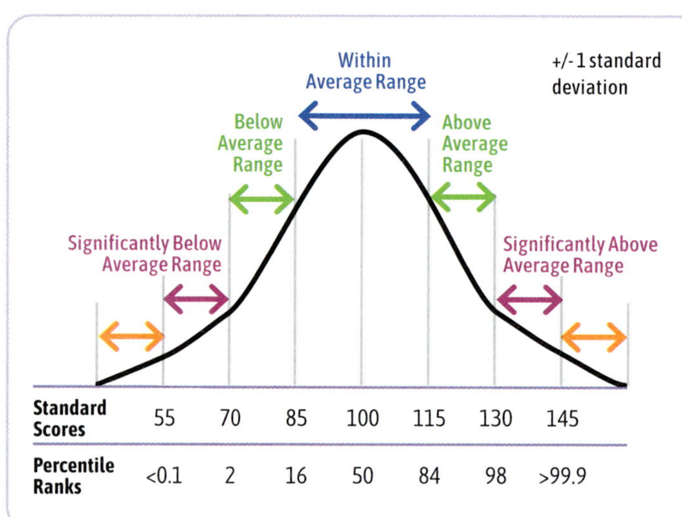

When raw scores are converted to various scales for interpretation, it is assumed that the distribution of scores is normal, meaning it fits a symmetrical, bell-shaped curve. In a normal distribution, 68 percent of the scores fall between one standard deviation below and one standard deviation above the mean. For example, many norm-referenced tests are converted to scales that have a mean of 100 and a standard deviation of 15. When you interpret a norm-referenced test, scores between 85 and 115 are considered average, scores between 70 and 85 are considered below average, and scores between 115 and 130 are considered above average. The chart on the previous page shows the corresponding stanines and percentile ranks. Confused? You're not alone. This is why we recommend sticking to raw scores that are easily interpreted.

Raw scores are converted by comparing each student's scores to the *norming sample*, or the group of students who took the test when the study was conducted, to create the various scales. The range of scores obtained by students in the norming sample is called the *distribution*. The average score across that range is called the *mean*. The *standard deviation* around the mean describes how closely clustered or spread apart the scores are from the mean, or average score. A large standard deviation means students' performance varied widely. A small standard deviation means students scored more similarly. Risk status cut scores on screening assessments should have small standard deviations because that means the score is more reliable and represents the average or typical student.

The chart on the next few pages provides a description, an example, and the main pros and cons of the common types of scores you will encounter.

Common Types of Scores

Type of Score	Description	Example	Pros and Cons
Raw Score	The number of items the student got correct; may be reported as a percent correct	You will likely encounter these scores on curriculum-embedded tests and CBM measures, such as Acadience Reading and DIBELS 8th Edition. Example: John scored 32. He was 85 percent correct.	**PRO:** Easy to understand **CON:** Scores can't be compared across tests.
Scale Score	The converted scores that use an arbitrarily chosen scale to represent students' performance Stanines, grade equivalents, and normal curve equivalents (described below) are all scale scores.	See below.	**PRO:** Enables comparison of scores across forms of the test, students, classes, schools, or school districts/school boards **CON:** Different raw scores can result in the same scale score, so these can be confusing to interpret, especially when trying to determine how much a student improved.

Common Types of Scores (cont.)

Type of Score	Description	Example	Pros and Cons
Stanine	The conversion of raw scores based on dividing a score distribution into nine equal segments In normal distributions, the highest (stanine 9) and lowest (stanine 1) contain about 4 percent of the scores and stanine 5 contains about 20 percent.	You'll likely encounter these scores on group-administered achievement tests like SAT-10, GRADE, and Terra Nova. Example: John scored at the 6th stanine, which is in the average range. Stanines 1–3 are below average and stanines 7–9 are above average.	**PRO:** The inexact nature of stanines conveys the lack of precision in educational measurement. **CON:** Each stanine contains different proportions of the score's distribution.
Grade Equivalent	The conversion of a raw score to a rough estimate of how well a student understands what was tested along a continuum across grades The score compares a student's score to an estimate of how well a student in another grade might do on the assessment.	You'll likely encounter these scores on reading achievement tests given by school psychologists, SLPs and outside professionals, and some computer-adaptive tests. Example: John received a grade equivalent score of 3.5. John is a second grader who earned as many points as students in the norm group who were in the fifth month of third grade.	**PRO:** None. These scores should not be used. **CON:** These scores are an easily misunderstood estimate, not a representation of what the student actually performed. They imply a level of precision and equivalent difficulty that isn't a reality.
Normal Curve Equivalent	The conversion of a raw score to a scale score representing relative position in a distribution of others who took the test	You'll likely encounter these scores on group reading achievement tests like the SAT-10, Terra Nova, and ITBS, and some computer-adaptive tests. Example: John received a NCE of 50, placing him in the middle of the scale between 1 (the lowest) and 99 (the highest).	**PRO:** Enables comparison across tests **CON:** These scores assume a normal distribution, which is seldom the case.
Standard Score (also called z-score)	The conversion of a raw score to show the number of standard deviations above or below the average score	You'll likely encounter these scores on reading achievement tests like Woodcock Reading Mastery or KTEA-3. Example: John scored 117, which is slightly more than one standard deviation above the average score.	**PRO:** Shows a student's rank compared to other students by indicating how far above or below the mean a student scored. Useful for comparing student performance across tests **CON:** They are less straightforward than raw scores, with the potential for misinterpretation.

Common Types of Scores (cont.)

Type of Score	Description	Example	Pros and Cons
Percentile or Percentile Rank	The relative position of a student within a group of other students who took the test In other words, this represents the percentage of students in the norm group who the student outperformed.	You'll likely encounter these scores on reading tests like Gray Oral Reading Test and CTOPP-2. Example: John scored at the 84th percentile, which means he scored better than 84 percent of the students in the norm group.	**PRO:** Enables comparison across students **CON:** They don't tell you if the score represents having enough of the skill to be an okay reader in the future.
RIT (Rasch Unit) Score	The conversion of a raw score that represents continuous progress by estimating the difficulty level of questions a student is likely to answer with 50 percent accuracy, regardless of their grade	You'll likely encounter these scores on screening tests, such as STAR Early Literacy and MAP Growth. Example: John's RIT score was 315, which means he is likely to answer correctly about 50 percent of the items calibrated to be at this RIT level.	**PRO:** Enables comparison across grades and over time **CON:** These scores are difficult to understand, and their creation is not made public. The scores can't be used to group students or plan instruction.

7. Interpretation: Understanding Results

There are three common ways to interpret test scores: norm-referenced, criterion-referenced, and individually referenced.

Norm-Referenced Score Interpretation

One way to interpret test scores is to compare a student's score to the norming sample. These are called *norm-referenced interpretations* because they compare students to a sample of other students who took the same test. They are useful if you need to know how a student scored compared to other students of the same age or in the same grade.

Criterion-Referenced Score Interpretation

A second way to interpret test scores is to compare a student's score to a minimum threshold of performance, sometimes called a benchmark. These *criterion-referenced interpretations* have an advantage over norm-referenced interpretations because they help you to determine if a student has reached a predetermined, minimum level of performance, regardless of how their performance compares to other students.

> **Burning Question**
>
> ***What's the difference between the terms standardized and norm-referenced?***
>
> It is easy to confuse the terms *standardized* and *norm-referenced*. *Standardized* refers to the way a test is given and *norm-referenced* refers to the way it is interpreted. While it is true that a test can be both standardized and norm-referenced, norm-referenced tests must be given exactly the same way each time, whereas standardized tests can be interpreted in norm-referenced, criterion-referenced, or individually referenced ways. DIBELS 8th Edition and Acadience Reading are examples of standardized tests that generate raw scores that can be interpreted in norm-referenced, criterion-referenced, or individually referenced ways. The criterion-referenced benchmark goals provided by the test authors are more useful for interpreting universal screening and progress-monitoring scores than norm-referenced interpretations.

What Is a Benchmark Goal?

One of the greatest assessment innovations of the twentieth century was the creation of benchmark goals. Building on the work of earlier experts who used Curriculum-Based Measures (CBMs) to track students' progress (e.g, Tindal, 2017; Fuchs et al., 1993), Roland Good and Ruth Kaminski published the first benchmark goals for their test originally called DIBELS,* now called Acadience Reading. Before that time, teachers could only compare scores to national or local norms which varied year to year and school to school. With benchmark goals, teachers know what to expect because the scores for each grade are the same each year.

You may have heard that a benchmark is a high bar for performance, but in fact, a benchmark goal is the minimum score that predicts adequate reading performance in the future, on Acadience and other reading assessments. The benchmark goal is the "lowest level of okay" performance. Students who score at or above the benchmark goal have about an 80 to 90 percent chance of being okay readers in the future. Students who score below benchmark have about a 40 to 60 percent chance and students who score well below benchmark have only a 10 to 20 percent chance. (Note that these numbers reflect the predictions if instruction doesn't change—we have the power to change instruction and change the odds!) Because the benchmark goal represents the minimally acceptable score, we should aim for the above benchmark goal where the student's odds of future reading health are 90 to 99 percent. In addition to being straightforward and easy to interpret for universal screening, benchmark goals serve as research-based minimum cut points for screening decisions and targets for setting progress-monitoring goals because reaching them improves a student's odds of proficient reading.

Now, other assessments, such as DIBELS 8th Edition and FastBridge, offer benchmark goals that are minimum thresholds. Some assessments, such as

*The test now called DIBELS 8th Edition is unrelated to DIBELS Next or any prior edition. For more information, search online "Acadience Reading Joint Legal Statement, DIBELS Next."

aimswebPlus, the Measures of Academic Progress (MAP), and the Standard Testing and Reporting (STAR), report scores relative to benchmarks, but those goals are national norms, not research-derived minimum cut points for risk. Don't assume the term *benchmark* means a minimum score that predicts future risk. Check with the test publisher about how it uses the term *benchmark*.

We recommend criterion-referenced early literacy tests for universal screening and progress monitoring. They are quick to administer and you can determine how each of your students is performing in essential skill areas compared with a minimum threshold of performance for their grade level. This information allows you to teach early and with the level of intensity that can change future reading outcomes, which is the whole point of doing universal screening. Screening tests that are interpreted only with norms are less useful. What good is it to know if a student scored higher than others in their school, district, or country if you still don't know if that score represents adequate skills now and predicts adequate reading in the future?

What Is a Composite Score?

A *composite score* summarizes a collection of scores on screening measures. It is more reliable, valid, and predictive than any individual measure score. The composite score is calculated using scores from all required measures for that grade and period of time (e.g., middle of the year in second grade). Kate likes to think of it as the "grand total"—though the math is a bit more complicated than that! For example, the formula used with Acadience Reading combines scores in a way that each one is weighted so it contributes equally to the composite.

While information on specific measures is really important for determining student strengths and needs, the composite score provides an overall, comprehensive total that is the best indicator of general risk for that student. Looking at composite scores for a class (or beyond) also gives us good information about general instruction and support needed.

While there are many reporting systems to do your calculations for you, it's still good professional learning to have a clear idea where the score is coming from. When we lead training, we make sure to have participants hand-calculate a couple of composite score examples for better understanding.

Individually Referenced Score Interpretation

A third way to interpret test scores involves comparing a student's current performance to his or her past performance. These are called *individually referenced interpretations* because they compare students to their own past performance. This interpretation is especially useful for looking at growth over time, such as when conducting progress monitoring and particularly with a student who has been tested with unapproved accommodations so there is a basis for comparison.

> **Burning Question**
>
> ***What do we mean by a "measure"?***
>
> A measure is another word for a specific component of assessment. Phoneme Segmentation Fluency, Nonsense Word Fluency, and Oral Reading Fluency are all examples of measures you'd likely find in criterion-referenced CBM assessments.

Here is an example that illustrates how the same score can be interpreted from all three frames of reference. Let's say a student scored 118 on a test (his raw score). Compared to other students in his grade around the country, he scored at the 55th percentile (norm-referenced interpretation). This score was below benchmark, meaning it was too low to predict reaching future reading outcomes without support (criterion-referenced interpretation). However, compared to the last three times the student took the same test, this score was the highest yet (individually referenced interpretation). When it comes to early literacy, criterion-referenced and individually referenced interpretations are most useful.

In Closing, Remember...

Decisions about the formality of the assessment, its technical properties, and how it is interpreted depend on who will use the information, if the information is needed for one student or for many, and if the information will be used only now or also in the future.

We know that there was likely a lot of new learning in this chapter, but we hope this knowledge helps you to not only select tests and interpret results, but also to interpret results of tests given to your students by other education professionals.

In Chapter 3, we focus on Multi-Tiered Systems of Support (MTSS) and give you an idea of how your role on the team fits in the big picture of effective reading instruction.

The Big Picture: Creating Data-Driven Systems for School-Wide Reading Improvement

Reading assessment is a key component of school systems that gets results. Improving reading outcomes starts with assessments that identify what students know and what they need to learn. Unfortunately, though, in the United States and Canada, too many students are struggling to read and too many teachers are feeling the pressure to solve that problem. The solution lies in efficient use of reading assessments to create structures for prevention and early intervention.

We included this chapter because we believe it's beneficial for you, the frontline educator, to see the big picture of what a successful system looks like, so you can maximize your classroom contributions, and perhaps even convince some of your colleagues and leaders to follow suit!

What Is MTSS?

Multi-Tiered System of Support (MTSS) is a framework for improving reading outcomes. It involves school teams administering assessments and using data from them to design evidence-based tiers of support that result in all students reading for meaning. The MTSS framework allows educators to bring the science of reading to their school in a way that ensures it will be embraced, implemented, and sustained over time for the benefit of all students.

Here are some signs your school might need MTSS:

- You've completed training on the science of reading, but results aren't improving.
- You've purchased new programs, but results aren't improving.
- You've conducted universal screening, but results aren't improving.

While training, programs, and screening data are important, none of them is a standalone solution. Schools are complex systems, and improving reading outcomes can be challenging.

MTSS enables educators to address that complexity by viewing each student in the context of the multiple, overlapping systems. What do we mean by that? We mean the family system, which includes home language and culture; the classroom system, which includes the curriculum, instructional materials, schedule, grouping formats, and classroom management; and the broader school system, which includes the bell schedule, professional development, budget, policies, and support for students who are struggling. As a teacher, you have control of the classroom system, and you can be an advocate for the school system. You're in a powerful position!

When students have reading difficulties, those systems can be possible levers for change. More importantly, they can be organized in a way that prevents reading difficulties. Think about your own class. If you have just one struggling reader, you can approach helping him or her as an individual. But if you have two, five, or even 10 struggling readers, wouldn't it be more efficient to solve the problem by improving aspects of your classroom system? If you and the teacher next door each have five struggling readers, wouldn't it be more efficient to accelerate their progress together by engaging in grade-level or school-level conversations that enable your team to maximize teaching time and resources? Schools that make lasting reading improvement see the big picture and plan for systemic improvements.

Key Components of MTSS

It's not unusual for a school to put its own twist on MTSS, but all variations share the following components, even if they go by different names:

- School-Wide Assessments
- Tiered Instruction
- Leadership and Teaming
- Collaborative Improvement Cycle
- Professional Development and Coaching

School-Wide Assessments

To build an MTSS that improves reading outcomes for all students, you must select assessments based on answers to the following questions.

Which students and systems need help?

Prevention and intervention are foundational goals of MTSS. Early action requires early detection of potential difficulties that interfere with students' reading progress. **Universal screening assessments** help us accomplish that. (See Chapter 4 for more information.)

What should be taught and how?

Prevention and early intervention require precise instructional moves. Because universal screening assessments are brief and don't always pinpoint what to teach next, **diagnostic assessments** are sometimes needed after screening. They provide details about the skill areas in which a student struggled during screening which lead directly to next steps for instruction. (See Chapter 5 for more information.)

Is the instruction working?

Prevention and early intervention require real-time monitoring of student performance. **Progress-monitoring assessments** are brief, repeatable indicators of essential skills. Often, they are different forms of the same assessments used for universal screening. Teachers often graph the results for visual feedback about the effectiveness of their instruction and intervention. (See Chapter 6 for more information.)

Did the instruction work?

Prevention and early intervention demand ongoing action, reflection, and revision. **Outcome assessments** enable us to look back at student performance and decide whether to repeat the same instruction in the future. (See Chapter 7 for more information.)

Tiered Instruction

Your school-wide assessment system forms the basis for designing the instructional systems, or tiers, needed to reach universal literacy. Three key research findings should guide your reading-improvement efforts within the MTSS framework (Good & Kaminski, 1996; Fien et al., 2021; Simmons et al., 2000; Torgesen, 2002):

1. Prevention is possible and early intervention is essential.
2. All students can succeed, but not with the same kind or amount of instruction.
3. Efficient resource allocation supports all students to succeed.

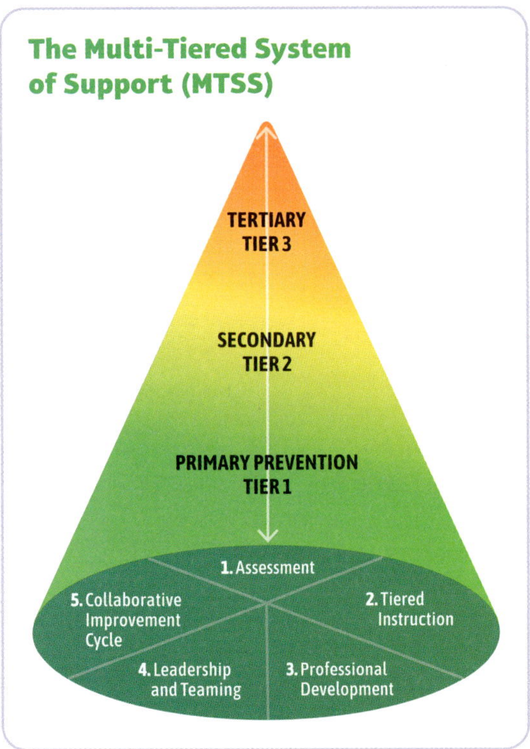

Those findings are at the heart of the diagram at left, which shows the efficient use of resources in layers of instruction and intervention that support all students to be skilled readers.

All students can reach minimum reading expectations, but each one may require different kinds and amounts of instruction. To reach that goal, instruction in the regular classroom, Tier 1 instruction, has to be effective enough to get the vast majority of students on track, leaving only a small, manageable number who need intervention, or Tier 2 or Tier 3 instruction, to get on track. Results from universal screening and diagnostic assessment inform what the tiers of classroom reading instruction and intervention look like at each grade. The chart below describes each tier of support and how to evaluate its effectiveness.

Learn more about Tier I from Stephanie here.

Three Tiers in MTSS

	Tier 1	Tier 2	Tier 3
Purpose	Prevent reading failure Minimize number of students who need intervention	Accelerate progress and catch students up to grade level	Accelerate progress and catch students up to grade level
Students	All	Some	A few
Characteristics	Research-aligned scope and sequence and instructional approaches Designed to match the needs of all students (English learners, gifted, students with disabilities) Whole group and small group	Additional time Aligned to Tier 1 Small group More frequent progress monitoring	Additional time Aligned to Tiers 1 and 2 Small group More frequent progress monitoring
Measure of Effectiveness	Approximately 80 percent reach goals with Tier 1 alone	80–100 percent who get Tier 1 and 2 reach goals	80–100 percent who get Tier 1 and 3 reach goals

The tiers represent all resources in a school, not just the instructional programs. For example, building the tiers requires careful decisions about daily operations, such as how much time to schedule for reading instruction, how adult resources are allocated, what professional development to offer, and how to group for instruction. Because the tiers represent doses of aligned instruction, not three different programs (which is a common misconception), it is important to plan a cohesive system of supports. Students who are behind need more time each day in instruction that aims to close their skill gaps so they make accelerated progress and reach end-of-grade standards. The priorities include preventing reading problems before the end of first grade and remediating reading difficulties early in each grade.

Learn more about aligning programs from Stephanie here.

Leadership and Teaming

Using assessment results to construct tiers of support is the work of teams at all levels of the school system (district/board, school, grade, and student).

At the heart of MTSS is acknowledging that reading results won't improve unless classroom reading instruction improves. The job of everyone in a school system is to create conditions for teachers to deliver optimal reading instruction. You may find that your school's current tiers of support are not effective and not getting all students to minimal levels of reading proficiency. This is the hard work of building an MTSS! Results can improve quickly when all educators in the system are working together.

The chart on the following page details MTSS teaming structures you might want to consider.

Burning Question

Is MTSS the same as RtI?

If you haven't heard of MTSS, perhaps you are familiar with Response to Intervention (RtI). Although the models are similar, RtI was often implemented in a narrow way that involved a set of meetings and forms to move students from Tier 1 to Tier 2 and to Tier 3. In some places, RtI was used to determine special education eligibility, which is part of MTSS. In many cases, RtI implementation didn't lead to the kinds of systemic changes that define MTSS, which made it an ineffective approach. MTSS is a school-improvement framework in which teams of educators use data to identify and remove barriers to effective teaching and learning.

Teaming Structures

Team	Purpose	Members	Data Sources	Teacher's Role	Meeting Frequency
Student-Level Team	Write a reading improvement plan	• School administrator(s) • Teacher(s) • Relevant school personnel • Parents/guardians and community members	• Instruction and intervention data • An individual student's screening, diagnostic, and progress-monitoring data	• Describe concerns about the student's reading performance • Share data • Contribute to planning future instruction • Provide parents/guardians with ways to provide support at home	As needed
Grade-Level Team	Inform and implement the school reading improvement plan	• School administrator(s) • Teacher(s) • Special educator(s) • All staff who serve students in the grade	• Instruction and intervention data • Percent at benchmark on screening • Diagnostic assessment data • Progress-monitoring data	• Provide class-level data • Offer input on what is needed to improve classroom reading instruction and grade-level interventions in terms of schedule, materials, PD, coaching, staffing, and family communication	Weekly
Building-Level Team	Inform and implement a school improvement plan aligned with the district/board improvement plan	• Building and district/board administrator(s) • Representatives from teachers in each grade, and from other roles such as coaches, interventionists, related services, union, special education • Representatives from families and community members	• Instruction and intervention data • Percent at benchmark on screening • Diagnostic assessment data • Progress-monitoring data	• Provide grade-level data • Offer input on what the grade needs to improve classroom reading instruction and interventions in terms of schedule, materials, PD, coaching, staffing, and family communication	Every other week

Teaming Structures (cont.)

Team	Purpose	Members	Data Sources	Teacher's Role	Meeting Frequency
District/ Board- Level Team	Use district/ board data to identify and remove barriers to better reading outcomes by making decisions on policy, funding, staffing, PD, and materials Write a district or board reading improvement plan	• Superintendent • Administrators, including representatives from each school and district/board • Teachers, including representatives from each school and from other roles such as coaches, interventionists, related service providers, union representatives, special educators • Representatives from students' families and the community	• Percent at benchmark on universal screening in each grade at each school • Percent who caught up with Tier 2 and 3 intervention • Percent who exit special education	• Provide school-level data • Offer input on what the school needs to improve classroom reading instruction and interventions in terms of schedule, materials, PD, coaching, staffing, and family communication	Monthly

Certainly, parents and other guardians are essential members of the team, at all levels, including at the building level and district/board level so that action plans and decisions reflect their perspectives and have their support.

Teachers should serve on teams at all levels, too. Their voices need to be heard when decisions are made throughout the system. After all, teachers are often champions for MTSS, as they are usually the first to recognize the need for prevention, early intervention, and reading improvement. In districts where no formal team structure exists, honoring the teacher perspective still matters. In Kate's district, the coaches, consultant, and superintendent acknowledge her expertise and value to the system both privately and publicly, even though she is in a classroom role.

Collaborative Improvement Cycle

You may already serve on teams in your school. What makes MTSS effective is the decision-making structure used during team meetings, which is called the Collaborative Improvement Cycle (CIC) (Brown & Stollar, 2025), an extension of collaborative problem-solving (Curtis & Stollar, 2002; Deno, 2002; Gutkin & Curtis, 1990; Tilly et al., 1999). While it is possible to use the steps of the cycle described in this section as an individual teacher, the most powerful outcomes occur when the process is used by collaborative teams, where each team member is an equal partner in improving reading outcomes. As a teacher, you play an integral role on these teams!

The CIC is the step-by-step process of using assessment information to create action plans and evaluate their impact. Without it, you might make unwise decisions, such as giving assessments without fully understanding a student's difficulties, or interpreting data in a way that leaves you with unanswered questions. Whatever the decision, you are wasting time and not getting results.

The same four steps of the CIC apply, whether you are designing reading instruction for an individual student (student-level problem-solving) or all students (system-level problem-solving).

- Step 1: Gap Identification
- Step 2: Gap Analysis
- Step 3: Action Planning
- Step 4: Outcome Analysis

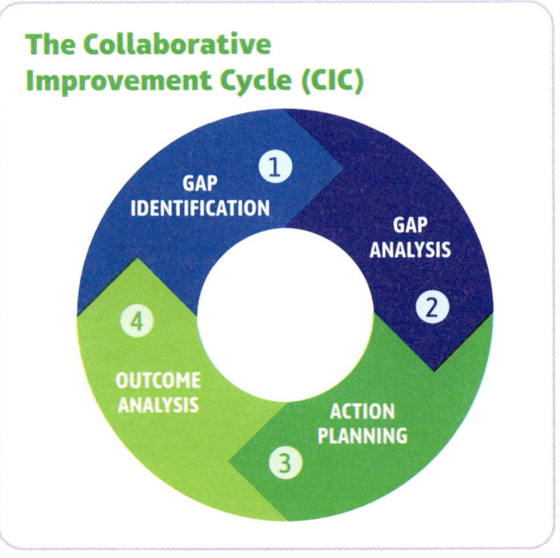

Throughout this book, you will see examples of both system-level and school-level improvement cycles in action. We explain each step next and provide a chart on page 49 illustrating each step for a student and for a system.

The chart below appears in Chapters 4, 5, 6, and 7 to orient you to the connection between the step of the CIC and the purposes of assessment.

Step	Key Questions	Assessment Purpose
1. Gap Identification	• Which students and systems need help? • What is the gap between actual and desired outcomes?	Universal Screening
2. Gap Analysis	• What should be taught and how? • Why is the gap happening?	Diagnostic Assessment
3. Action Planning	• What is the plan to close the gap?	
4. Outcome Analysis	• Is the instruction working? • Did the instruction work?	Progress Monitoring Outcome Assessment

Step 1: Gap Identification

Identifying the gap between actual and desired performance enables you to plan and implement reading instruction that gets results. In MTSS, a gap or problem is defined as the difference between desired outcome and actual performance. It is most helpful to define reading problems in observable and measurable ways. For example, rather than generally saying a student in grades 3–5 has a reading comprehension problem, it would be more precise and useful to say the student isn't understanding grade-level text because he or she can't yet decode multisyllabic words.

This is different from how reading problems are typically defined. Often, we hear educators defining reading difficulties in terms of internal student factors (e.g., the student has a processing disorder or dyslexia, or we see them as lazy or immature); factors related to prior instruction (e.g., assessing skills that haven't been taught); factors related to home and family life (e.g., parents/family members are not supportive or don't value education), or factors that aren't specific enough to inform instruction (e.g., a reading comprehension problem or ADHD). We encourage you to focus on identifying problems that are within your control to change.

When you first start using the CIC, you may be tempted to move quickly to Step 3, Action Planning. But try to resist that temptation. If you don't clearly and correctly define the gap, you run the risk of wasting time solving the wrong problem.

Step 2: Gap Analysis

Gap analysis is the bridge between the observable and measurable statement of the gap or problem and effective reading instruction, and, like gap identification, it should not be rushed. It involves asking questions about your students as readers and selecting assessments to answer them. The complexity of reading drives home this point. There are many reasons why students don't understand what they read, including low vocabulary, lack of general content knowledge, difficulty decoding, or lack of text-reading fluency. If we don't define and analyze the problem in the right way, we won't find the solution.

One of the first questions to ask is, "Was the low performance a fluke?" We call this "validating need for support." Validating the need for support involves ruling out simple reasons for low performance, such as the student having a bad day or being sick, assessor error, or testing in a noisy environment. You don't want to plan an intervention if the screening results don't truly represent what the student can and cannot do.

Once you are sure there isn't an easy explanation for the low performance, you can move into generating questions about why the gap occurred and collecting any additional data needed to determine the root cause. Assessment questions lead to hypotheses that can be tested with assessments. The hypothesis that seems to be the reason for the identified gap between expected and actual performance becomes what the action plan is written to resolve.

The results of the assessments during gap analysis lead to a hypothesis about why the gap is occurring. The hypothesis leads to a plan for reading improvement—for the student or the system.

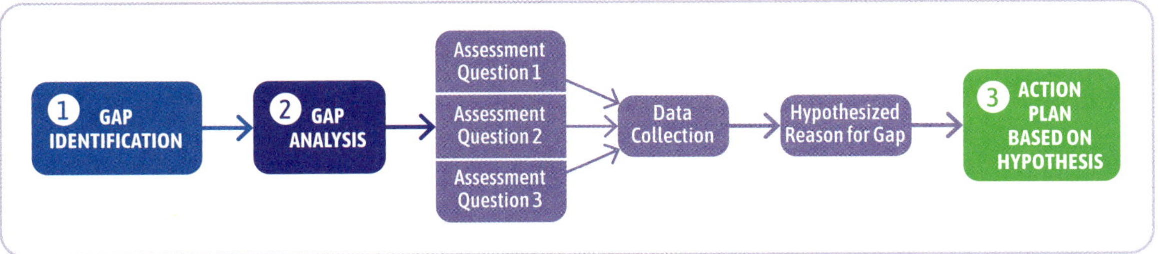

Step 3: Action Planning

Once you have a hypothesis of why the gap between expected and actual performance is occurring, craft a plan to act on it to improve reading performance. Reading improvement action plans include determining specific tasks, identifying who will do each task, mapping out a timeline, articulating a plan for progress monitoring, and setting a goal for the future.

This is where all of your assessment data and your knowledge of evidence-based instruction come together. Linking instruction to student needs is one of the most effective actions you can take. We encourage you to lean into the content in Chapter 8. The more detail you can include in the plan, the more effectively it will be implemented and the more likely you will be to see success. Just be sure the plan is realistic and doable. For example, if you are on your fourth principal in two years and adopting a new math program, and two out of three first-grade teachers will be on maternity leave, this might not be the year to implement a new reading assessment.

The space between knowing better and doing better is filled with the many realities of school life. Rather than ignoring reality, we recommend embracing and planning for it. The best intervention and action plans include support for doing what you planned (time, coaching, materials, etc.), not assuming the plan will be implemented. Remember, the CIC process in MTSS is about contextualizing reading science within the reality of your school, not giving up or hoping for magic bullets.

Step 4: Outcome Analysis

You've done the hard work of linking assessment results with research-aligned instruction, and putting your plan into action. Now, sit back and celebrate the results!

- If you met your goals, the next step could be moving on to the next concern on the list, fading the intensity of the intervention, or setting a new, higher goal for performance.
- If you didn't meet your goals, the next step could be revising the action plan, doing additional gap analysis, or revisiting the gap identification.

In Chapter 7, we go deeper into outcome assessment, and in Chapter 8, we elaborate on how to review progress-monitoring data and establish next steps.

The chart below illustrates the steps of the CIC for Ollie, a first grader, and for all first graders in his school. Each step of the CIC is illustrated with the assessments used and a student-level and system-level example.

CIC in Action

Step	Assessment	Student-Level Example	System-Level Example
Gap Identification	Universal Screening	Ollie should be able to segment phonemes at a rate of at least 40 per minute, but his score is 37. He should be able to match sounds to letters at a rate of 27 per minute and read at least one whole word, but his letter-sound score is 21 and he reads 0 whole words.	At the beginning of first grade, 100 percent of students should be able to segment phonemes in spoken words but only 77 percent of students met these expectations.
Gap Analysis	Diagnostic Assessment	Ollie can blend phonemes and identify initial phonemes but can't segment all sounds in words. He knows common sounds for 6 letters.	Most of the students can blend phonemes and they know letter sounds. The teachers have had training in how to teach phonemic awareness. They have a research-based phonics program that includes phonemic awareness. There isn't enough time in the schedule to get through the whole program, so they have skipped parts.
Action Planning		Teach segmenting phonemes, letter name, letter sound, blending, and how to write the letters explicitly and systematically.	The grade-level team develops a plan to minimize transitions to free up time to complete the whole program.
Outcome Analysis	Progress Monitoring Outcome Assessment	Implementation data, such as a checklist noting the percentage of steps of the instructional routine that were implemented. Progress monitoring toward the goal of 40 on PSF.	1. Percentage of instructional steps that were implemented. 2. Percentage of students who met progress-monitoring goals. 3. Percentage of students who met benchmark goals at middle-of-year screening.

If thinking strategically about reading concerns is new to you, you're not alone! We find that using the CIC is missing from most schools, even from ones that claim to use MTSS. This is definitely a topic for ongoing professional development and coaching. It is possible to efficiently reach reading improvement goals when everyone is thinking about issues the same way and using the same approach to using data during meetings.

Teamwork Makes the Dream Work

If you are the only one in your school working on reading improvement, we applaud you! You can use the CIC to be more targeted and efficient with designing interventions for your students. But we encourage you to expand the use of this approach to the work you do with others. As the John Maxwell expression in the section heading above implies, when all educators in the system are approaching problems in the same way, we can reach our goals much faster.

Let's be real: Collaborating with other educators is not always easy! Sometimes it feels safer and more comfortable to close your door and do what you can on your own. Here are some practical strategies for moving toward a more collaborative approach:

- Find another educator in your school who is interested in improving reading outcomes.
- Introduce the structure of the CIC into existing team meetings.
- Obtain training and coaching on the use of the CIC.
- Implement consistent meeting agendas and team roles that support the steps of the CIC.
- Distribute agendas before meetings and notes after meetings.
- Distribute and communicate which decisions will be made collaboratively and which will be made by administrators.

Parents as Equal Partners

Parents and other guardians are essential members of MTSS teams. You may already have parents and guardians participating on teams that involve their own child. To be fully contributing members of their child's team, parents and other family members need to be prepared ahead of time with information about the assessments and instructional materials that are being used. They should be familiar with the steps of CIC as they will be used to design and evaluate interventions for their child.

The assessments we suggest in this book, particularly Curriculum-Based Measures, can help to facilitate communication among teachers, parents/guardians, and students because, as Hosp and Hosp (2007) write, "the information collected using CBM is not unlike what the teacher is teaching, the student is learning, and the parents see sent home." Standardized use of progress-monitoring graphs provides visual support to help parents and guardians understand their children's growth in reading as well.

It is possible you haven't thought about the value of preparing parents to participate on your building- and district-level leadership teams. This requires a level of vulnerability and commitment that can have tremendous payoff in terms of commitment to change and efficient decision-making. When parents/guardians are treated as equal partners in making decisions about improving reading outcomes, schools avoid errors such as alienating parents and guardians or having to abandon plans due to resistance.

Professional Development and Coaching

Ongoing improvement in reading outcomes requires professional development and coaching for all educators at the school, not just classroom teachers, and for parents and other community members. In addition to the science of reading, training should focus on how to select and give assessments and interpret results, how to select and implement instructional programs, and how to collaborate in teams to use assessment results to solve problems.

Castillo and colleagues (2024) explored the type of professional learning that helps educators to implement key components of MTSS. Their analysis of 46 studies revealed that educators had positive experiences when MTSS implementation included ongoing, job-embedded professional learning and coaching, particularly when facilitated by trusted, empowering leaders. These are the ideal conditions every school should strive for. If that's not happening yet where you are, rest assured, we've packed as much professional development as possible into this book!

In Closing, Remember...

Schools are complex systems. Without a strong vision and leadership, the number of students in your classroom and school who fail to read proficiently is likely to stay the same year after year. Whether you are that visionary leader or someone who supports him or her, MTSS provides a framework for implementing the science of reading to improve outcomes. Real and lasting change can happen by identifying and analyzing the gap between desired and actual performance, creating and implementing a plan, and reviewing results until you reach your goals for each and every student. Wondering what that looks like in a real classroom? We've got you covered in the book's next part, where we take you step-by-step through the four types of assessment and how to make them work for you!

CHAPTER 4

Universal Screening

Which Students and Systems Need Help?

Research is clear on the value of prevention and early intervention (Al Otaiba et al., 2011; Fien et al., 2021; Foorman et al., 1998; Torgesen et al., 2002). The purpose of screening is to identify which students are struggling or are predicted to struggle in the future so instruction, even intensive intervention, can be provided early enough to change the prediction. When it comes to reading, the old adage holds true: An ounce of prevention is worth a pound of cure.

We see screening serving two important functions:

- Finding students who are at risk or struggling readers
- Identifying instructional systems that are not meeting the needs of all students

Teachers use screening assessments to measure the literacy health of each of their students and also to evaluate the effectiveness of the instruction in their class, grade, and school.

Stephanie "When I started in education, we had to rely on teachers to refer students for reading support. Teachers are generally pretty accurate at identifying which students are struggling, but let's face it, there are limits to the number of students any teacher is going to refer for intervention, which means some students were not served each year. Now that we have universal screening assessments, we can scan student performance in an entire school and know who is struggling and who may struggle if we don't intervene. Universal screening is indeed a game changer!"

UNIVERSAL SCREENING

ANALOGY: Thermometer for a wellness check (Everyone gets screened, regardless of symptoms.)

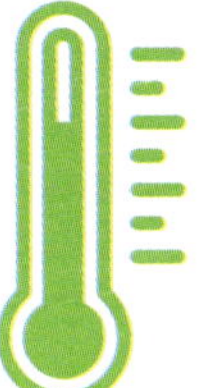

Step	Key Questions	Assessment Purpose
1. Gap Identification	• Which students and systems need help? • What is the gap between actual and desired outcomes?	Universal Screening
2. Gap Analysis	• What should be taught and how? • Why is the gap happening?	Diagnostic Assessment
3. Action Planning	• What is the plan to close the gap?	
4. Outcome Analysis	• Is the instruction working? • Did the instruction work?	Progress Monitoring Outcome Assessment

What Are Characteristics of a Quality Screener?

To identify a quality screener, look for these characteristics:

- **It is given to all students.** We want to know who might have a temperature (i.e., be at risk), and the parts of the tiered instructional system that need improvement (Tier 1, Tier 2, Tier 3).
- **It is brief.** Screening measures give us a quick snapshot of a student's essential literacy skills. You'll find the word "fluency" in the name of almost every screening measure, because when assessing skills, it's not just about accuracy; research tells us that rate matters, too, which is why almost all of these measures are timed, usually for one minute (Fuchs et al., 2001; Nathan & Stanovich, 1991; Perfetti & Hart, 2002; VanDerHeyden & Solomon, 2023). We want essential skills to be so automatic that they are "overlearned" to free up working memory so students can focus on the text's meaning when reading.
- **It is standardized.** A screener is given and scored in exactly the same way by every person who gives it, every time it's given (more on standardization of screeners in a moment).

- **It is predictive.** A screener predicts future reading outcomes. It tells you if students' performance today predicts they will be okay as readers in the future so you can work to make sure every student reaches that goal.
- **It provides student-level and system-level information.** We want data not only to tell us about the performance of individual students, but also to gauge the effectiveness of our classroom instruction. Does our Tier 1 or core instruction get at least 80 percent of students to grade-level expectations, leaving a maximum of 20 percent who may need Tier 2 or 3 in addition to Tier 1 to reach grade-level performance?

Learn more about using screening data from Stephanie here.

- **It serves as an indicator of essential literacy skills.** Research has converged on the importance of five essential skill areas for proficient reading:
    - phonemic awareness
    - the alphabetic principle and basic phonics
    - vocabulary and oral language
    - text-reading fluency
    - reading comprehension

  If those are the must-have skills, they should be the focus of any screening assessment. (Castles et al., 2018; Snow et al., 1998)
- **It is administered by a trained adult.** Ideally, a trained adult administers screeners face-to-face with children, as opposed to children taking them on a computer. There is a lot to be learned by watching and listening to students respond during screening assessments!
- **It requires students to produce responses.** While some assessments require students to simply select (and potentially guess at!) correct responses (e.g., point to the picture, click on the letter), screening assessments require them to produce responses (e.g., say the phoneme, read the words), giving us a clearer idea of their skill level.

Note that screeners do not identify dyslexia; they identify reading difficulties or risk of future reading difficulties. Administering them isn't about labeling or tracking students. It's about targeting gaps as early as possible to provide students with intervention if necessary.

What Type of Assessments Work Best for Screening?

The types of tools that work best for universal screening in MTSS are called Curriculum-Based Measures (CBM). CBMs are brief (usually one minute) opportunities for teachers to sit with students and observe them performing tasks that are similar to what teachers do during reading instruction. CBMs started in the late 1970s as a way to provide teachers feedback for instructional decision-making. Through decades of research, they have evolved to the assessments used today, such as Acadience Reading K–6, DIBELS 8th Edition, FastBridge, and aimswebPlus.

CBMs have standardized directions, prompts, and scoring rules. They have been found to be reliable and valid indicators of fluency within the essential skill areas. Interpretation of CBM scores centers on using raw scores which teachers can easily translate into what to teach. The scores are most often interpreted in a criterion-referenced and individually referenced way, but local and national norms also can be used. Through the use of benchmark goals, the percentage of students who score okay on CBMs can be used to evaluate the effectiveness of the tiers of instruction. We recommend CBMs because they are ideal for use in the data-based decision-making that occurs during the Collaborative Improvement Cycle of MTSS.

Which Skills Should Be Screened?

The Simple View of Reading (Gough & Tunmer, 1986) reminds us that reading comprehension is the product of word recognition and language comprehension. Those domains provide fertile ground for assessment and offer a framework for thinking about what you're measuring during screening.

The chart on the next page provides an overview of common universal screening measures, which we will discuss in this chapter. See Chapter 5 (Diagnostic Assessment) for more on assessing language comprehension.

Common Screening Measures

Assessment	Word Recognition Measures		Reading Comprehension Measures
Acadience Reading K–6	• First Sound Fluency (FSF) • Phoneme Segmentation Fluency (PSF) • Nonsense Word Fluency (NWF)	• Spelling • Oral Reading Fluency (ORF) Accuracy	• Oral Reading Fluency (ORF) • Maze
DIBELS 8th Edition	• Phoneme Segmentation Fluency • Nonsense Word Fluency	• Oral Reading Fluency Accuracy	• Oral Reading Fluency • Maze
FastBridge	• Onset Sounds • Letter Sounds • Word Segmenting • Nonsense Words	• Sight Word Reading • Print Concepts • CBM Reading Accuracy	• CBM Reading
aimswebPlus	• Initial Sounds • Phoneme Segmentation • Nonsense Word Fluency • Word Reading Fluency	• Spelling • Print Concepts • Oral Reading Fluency Accuracy	• Oral Reading Fluency
easyCBM	• Phoneme Segmenting • Letter Sounds • Word Reading Fluency	• Passage Reading Fluency Accuracy	• Passage Reading Fluency

One of the most powerful advances in the last few decades is the ability to screen all students and know in minutes who is on track and who is not likely to meet future reading goals unless they get support. It is truly a crystal ball for teachers!

Gone are the days of expecting teachers to predict which students will struggle with reading and refer them to a team. With universal screening, we can know within the first few days of school which students in our class or grade need more support.

Kate "Out of all of the assessments we cover in this book, screening has been the complete game changer for my practice. It helps me to feel confident that my Tier 1 instruction is on track (as I write this, my latest data from the middle-of-year screener has 94 percent of my kindergarten students at benchmark) and also helps me identify areas of risk for specific students, giving me the opportunity to close gaps early and quickly. Those looking at school-wide and system-wide data can make informed—and life-changing—decisions based on screening results."

What If My School Uses a Computer Adaptive Test (CAT) for Screening?

A Computer Adaptive Test (CAT) is essentially an achievement test that is used to identify risk status. Students take it on a computer. The test includes many, many items that range from easy to hard. Students are first presented with items somewhere in the middle, or at a place indicated by their grade level, or perhaps based on a previous test score.

When students respond correctly to an item, they are presented with more difficult items, based on the performance of other students who previously took the test. When the students respond incorrectly to an item, they are presented with easier items. As such, each student has a unique path through the assessment.

Learn more about CATs from Stephanie here.

The computer software calculates the student's achievement level and offers recommendations for instructional topics, grouping arrangements, and risk status.

Why CBMs Over CATs?

While some researchers have found CATs to be adequate universal screening tools (Ball & O'Connor, 2016; Burns, 2023; Clemens et al., 2015; Truckenmiller et al., 2025), they are not our preferred screening tools and here is why. CATs are:

1. **Not brief**
   - Testing can take students away from instruction for 15–30 minutes or more.
2. **Not standardized**
   - Each student has his or her own unique path through individualized test items.
   - Two students with the same score may have received very different test items and therefore need very different instruction.
3. **Not always predictive of future reading health**
   - Screening accuracy varies across measures.
   - Some CATs are not optimally accurate for finding students who are at risk.

Examples of CATs

- MAP by NWEA
- aReading by FastBridge
- Star Early Literacy by Renaissance
- iReady

4. **Not useful for system-level planning**
    - Scores can't be aggregated for system-level planning and decision-making related to curriculum, instruction, and resource allocation because each student took different test items.
5. **Not indicators of the essential early literacy skills**
    - The test item banks may include thousands of items representing every grade-level standard rather than focusing on the essential skill areas (phonemic awareness, phonics, vocabulary, fluency, and reading comprehension).
6. **Not given by teachers**
    - Teachers don't have the opportunity to sit with students and listen to them produce responses demonstrating essential early literacy skills.
7. **Not production responses**
    - Multiple-choice items require choosing the right answer which is easier than producing the right answer.
8. **Not useful for planning instruction**
    - Reports often indicate a need for instruction in a skill when, in fact, the student may not have been presented with any items, or may have been presented with very few items, that tested that skill.
    - Scores are statistically manipulated and reported in a way that is difficult for most educators and parents and other guardians to understand.
    - Scores can't be used to inform instructional groups because of the issues noted above.
9. **Not designed for progress monitoring**
    - Most authors and publishers correctly advise against using CATs frequently.
    - Each time students are tested, they are presented with a different set of test items.
10. **Not appropriate for preK and kindergarten**
    - Fine motor skills are required to use the computer keyboard or mouse.

If you are required to use a CAT, you might also want to use the free version of Acadience Reading or DIBELS 8th Edition with some students for screening and progress monitoring.

What About Teacher-Made Screeners?

Do you need to use commercial assessments (such as CBMs or CATs) at all? Can't teachers just create something themselves or use an assessment created at the district level?

While there is definitely a time and place for teacher-created assessments (Kate is particularly proud of her set of end-of-unit tests for third-grade math), you've seen in this chapter that quality screening tools have to meet a LOT of important criteria to do the job we want them to do. Teacher- and district-created tools just can't check all those boxes. And why reinvent the wheel when there are existing (and possibly free!) high-quality tools for you?

Who Should Administer Screeners?

While Kate prefers to see classroom teachers administering their own screeners because of their familiarity with students and to develop a professional understanding of the process, what's most important is that those who administer screeners are properly trained, with refreshers happening on a regular basis.

Some schools and districts deploy assessment teams to screen large numbers of students, which can be more efficient, prevent added workload for teachers, and minimize classroom disruptions.

Stephanie prefers a hybrid model, where a substitute teacher or other adult covers the class so the classroom teacher can be part of the assessment team. That way, the teacher can handpick a few students to test, while the team tests the rest of the students.

The chart on the next page provides the pros and cons of various models of conducting universal screening.

Learn more about administering screeners from Stephanie here.

The Pros and Cons of Administration Options

Option	Pros	Cons
Classroom Teacher	• Personal knowledge of students (e.g., speech/dialect, accommodations) • More ownership of data and next steps • Professional learning	• Takes a big chunk of instructional time or teacher prep time to complete • Requires training all educators and providing refreshers
Hybrid: Teacher and Other Adult(s)	• Models shared responsibility for improving reading outcomes • Creates common language and data source across the school • Teachers can test students they are concerned about, ELs, students with articulation difficulties • Facilitates team use of the Collaborative Improvement Cycle to improve results	• More people to train • Must revisit the scoring rules over time to ensure fidelity • Requires communication across the team
School/ District Team	• Fewer people to train • Easier to release members to train/refresh • Extensive experience is quickly accumulated • Minimizes loss of instructional time • Less stress/pressure for classroom teachers	• Doesn't build capacity for classroom teachers • Easier for teachers to discount/ detach from results

Even if someone else administers screeners to your students, don't skip this chapter—and be sure you see more than the final data for your class. As we will discuss, response patterns and student-specific information are essential for your instructional planning. You need to go beyond the scores on a report and open up the booklet or pull up the scoring form details to see the behaviors behind the scores!

Learn more about preparing for screening from Stephanie here.

When Should You Screen Students?

Ideally, universal screening should occur at the beginning, middle, and end of the year. Early literacy skills and expectations change throughout the year so we can't just screen at the beginning of the year or even at the beginning and end because we might miss the students who fall into the risk zone at a critical time period. For example, at the beginning of the year in kindergarten, Acadience assesses only Letter Naming Fluency and First Sound Fluency. Students could appear to be safe from risk based on those assessments, but at middle-of-year, Phoneme Segmentation Fluency and Nonsense Word Fluency are also included. If you assumed a student didn't need to be screened again all year, you could miss important information about phonemic awareness and decoding, as well as lose precious months that could be used for intervention.

Teachers sometimes ask us if it is necessary to screen kindergarten or preK students at the beginning of the year. After all, this may be their first time in school! Keep in mind that screening is a window into the future. If the students are low-performing when they enter school, that information can help the staff put necessary supports in place. The earlier we know about needs, the earlier we can intervene.

Sometimes teachers fear screening in preK and kindergarten because they think the scores will be used for intervention outside the classroom. That's not the way we see it. Screening assessment is best used to inform classroom reading instruction in Tier 1.

We also don't "overreact" to the data we collect before students have received any instruction. One year, only 43 percent of Kate's preK students scored at benchmark on phonemic awareness at the beginning of the year. By the middle of the year, with only whole-group Tier 1 instruction, that number rose to 89 percent, leaving just a few students needing extra support in the second half of the year.

Keep It Fresh!

"You want to have screener refresher trainings throughout the year, and someone who can do fidelity checks to make sure the assessment is being administered properly and that we're all doing it the same way. Unless you talk to those involved, you may not realize there are some misunderstandings, and things can fall through the cracks when you're trying to train many educators at once."

—Renata Archie, *Reading Road Trip*: Season 1, Episode 6

We get similar questions about the necessity of continuing to screen all students across the year, especially students whose beginning-of-year scores are at or above the end-of-year expectations. Because we use universal screening to measure the health of the instructional system, not just individual students, all students should be represented in all three measurements. The results would be skewed if we took the high-performing students out of the mix in the middle and end of year. And importantly, all students should grow across the year, even high-performing students.

Standardization of Screeners

In Chapter 2, you learned all about the importance of standardized assessments. Here are a few tips to help ensure your screening process is standardized:

- **Begin with at-grade materials for screening, even when you expect they may be too difficult for a student.** Many published screening assessments have discontinue rules, so no student will be forced to spend even a full minute on a task that is too far above his or her skill level.
- **Recognize the importance of standard scoring notation.** When Kate first started using a screener, she was the only teacher in her school, and possibly her district, doing so. She tried to be efficient with her own little

> **Burning Question**
>
> ***I've heard screening isn't good for students because it focuses on deficits. True?***
>
> We get that question a lot, and Kate asked one of her expert *Reading Road Trip* podcast guests to respond.
>
> Kareem Weaver: "A screening is supposed to be an ounce of prevention. When you screen kids for reading difficulties, including things like dyslexia, what you're saying is we are not going to wait to fail. We're not going to wait until our children are struggling with their reading and the social-emotional trauma that comes with being a struggling reader… We're going to identify if there are gaps and we're going to do it now as opposed to waiting. That is a humane approach. That is a common sense approach… Oh, you're screening for a deficit? No, we're screening because we love the kids… Get them early. So the framing of asset versus deficit, I would just ask people to think about how soon do you want to identify what kids need?" (Season 2, Episode 5)

system of check marks and strike-throughs, which didn't matter because no one else saw the scoring booklets. Now that screening is being used district-wide and grade and school teams are gathering to look at results, it's really important to follow the procedures so that underlines and slashes mean the same thing, no matter the student.

- **Follow the directions for administering your screener, including the allowed prompts.** We can't use the discretion we had with previous reading assessments where we might rephrase a question, give more time, or provide a prompt that we just knew would do the trick with that child because if we do we are no longer comparing apples to apples and the benchmark scores lose their meaning.
- **Be aware of accommodations permitted by your screener, as well as their purpose.** For example, some screeners allow colored overlays or filters if regularly used as an accommodation for a visual impairment. Please note that research does not support the use of visual items like those as accommodations for students with dyslexia or other learning disabilities.
- **Never penalize students for pronunciation differences related to articulation, dialect, or speaking a first language other than English.**

Common Screening Measures: What You Need to Know

As noted earlier in the book, essential literacy skills flow from the Simple View of Reading. Screening all students three times a year provides an ongoing warning system about who is on track and who may need more support to reach reading goals. The following measures are included in most universal screening assessments because they indicate whether students are developing in essential skill areas, including phonemic awareness, phonics, text-reading fluency, and reading comprehension.

Many universal screening tools have measures with the same or similar names, such as Oral Reading Fluency. Keep in mind that each assessment has its own administration and scoring directions and its own set of goals. These are specific to each set of materials and should not be used interchangeably. You can't use the aimswebPlus passages with the FastBridge goals!

First Sound Fluency (Initial Sounds, Onset Sounds)

What Is It?

First Sound Fluency from Acadience Reading (and similar measures from other publishers) is an indicator of phonemic awareness used for screening in kindergarten and for progress monitoring older struggling readers. You read a list of words one at a time, and students are asked to identify and produce (say) the first sound (phoneme) in each word. This is typically a one-minute timed task. Not all screeners include this measure; some that do include picture prompts as well (e.g., aimswebPlus Initial Sounds and FastBridge Onset Sounds).

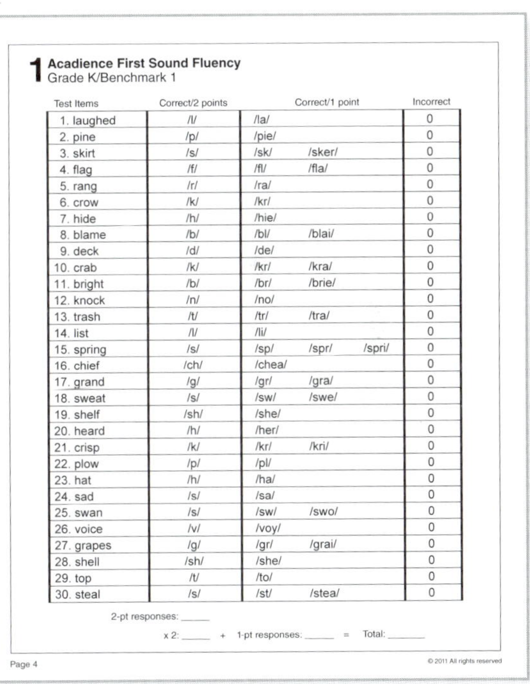

1 Acadience First Sound Fluency
Grade K/Benchmark 1

Test Items	Correct/2 points	Correct/1 point			Incorrect
1. laughed	/l/	/la/			0
2. pine	/p/	/pie/			0
3. skirt	/s/	/sk/	/sker/		0
4. flag	/f/	/fl/	/fla/		0
5. rang	/r/	/ra/			0
6. crow	/k/	/kr/			0
7. hide	/h/	/hie/			0
8. blame	/b/	/bl/	/blai/		0
9. deck	/d/	/de/			0
10. crab	/k/	/kr/	/kra/		0
11. bright	/b/	/br/	/brie/		0
12. knock	/n/	/no/			0
13. trash	/t/	/tr/	/tra/		0
14. list	/l/	/li/			0
15. spring	/s/	/sp/	/spr/	/spri/	0
16. chief	/ch/	/chea/			0
17. grand	/g/	/gr/	/gra/		0
18. sweat	/s/	/sw/	/swe/		0
19. shelf	/sh/	/she/			0
20. heard	/h/	/her/			0
21. crisp	/k/	/kr/	/kri/		0
22. plow	/p/	/pl/			0
23. hat	/h/	/ha/			0
24. sad	/s/	/sa/			0
25. swan	/s/	/sw/	/swo/		0
26. voice	/v/	/voy/			0
27. grapes	/g/	/gr/	/grai/		0
28. shell	/sh/	/she/			0
29. top	/t/	/to/			0
30. steal	/s/	/st/	/stea/		0

2-pt responses: ______

x 2: ______ + 1-pt responses: ______ = Total: ______

Page 4

First Sound Fluency from Acadience

Why Assess It?

- Students' ability to discern the first sound (phoneme) in a word is part of phonemic awareness, the understanding that spoken words are made up of individual sounds.
- Phonemic awareness is a strong predictor of future reading success, and is often the missing piece for students (even older ones) who are struggling readers.
- Phonemic awareness can be taught, and when students' phonemic awareness improves, so do their reading outcomes.

✗ **DON'T assume every phoneme is represented by one letter.** While your scoring sheet should make it clear what phonemes you're listening for as students respond to this task, it's good professional knowledge to be aware of the difference between a phoneme (sound) and a grapheme (letter). Some individual sounds are represented by more than one letter (e.g., digraphs such as *sh*, trigraphs such as *igh*, or even quadgraphs such as *eigh*). A letter can also represent more than one sound. More on that in Phoneme Segmentation Fluency, page 65.

Letter Naming Fluency

What Is It?

Letter Naming Fluency is a risk indicator, typically used for screening in kindergarten and the beginning of first grade. Because naming letters is not an essential early literacy skill, Acadience does not include goals or progress-monitoring materials for this measure. You provide students with a grid of letters (both uppercase and lowercase mixed together) and ask them to provide as many letter names as they can in one minute.

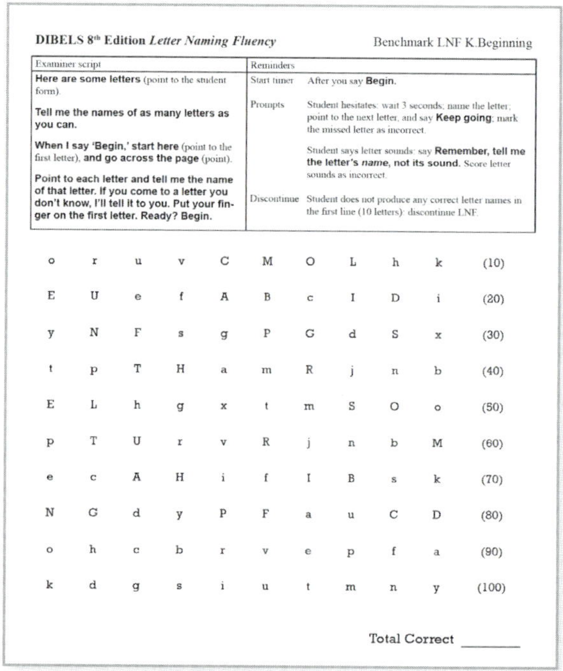

DIBELS 8th Edition ***Letter Naming Fluency*** Benchmark LNF K.Beginning

Examiner script	Reminders	
Here are some letters (point to the student form).	Start timer	After you say **Begin.**
Tell me the names of as many letters as you can.	Prompts	Student hesitates: wait 3 seconds; name the letter; point to the next letter, and say **Keep going**; mark the missed letter as incorrect.
When I say 'Begin,' start here (point to the first letter), **and go across the page** (point).		Student says letter sounds: say **Remember, tell me the letter's *name*, not its sound.** Score letter sounds as incorrect.
Point to each letter and tell me the name of that letter. If you come to a letter you don't know, I'll tell it to you. Put your finger on the first letter. Ready? Begin.	Discontinue	Student does not produce any correct letter names in the first line (10 letters): discontinue LNF.

o	r	u	v	C	M	O	L	h	k	(10)
E	U	e	f	A	B	c	I	D	i	(20)
y	N	F	s	g	P	G	d	S	x	(30)
t	p	T	H	a	m	R	j	n	b	(40)
E	L	h	g	x	t	m	S	O	o	(50)
p	T	U	r	v	R	j	n	b	M	(60)
e	c	A	H	i	f	I	B	s	k	(70)
N	G	d	y	P	F	a	u	C	D	(80)
o	h	c	b	r	v	e	p	f	a	(90)
k	d	g	s	i	u	t	m	n	y	(100)

Total Correct ________

DIBELS 8, University of Oregon

Why Assess It?

Letter Naming Fluency is not considered an essential early literacy skill. Technically, it's possible to learn to read without knowing the names of letters, which Kate has definitely seen happen. But being able to name letters fluently (not just accurately, but quickly) is a predictor of future reading success, and therefore an indicator of possible risk if students don't have that skill.

TIPS

✔ **DO remember the prompts to read verbatim when students skip letters or say the sound instead of the name.**

✔ **DO allow students to use a ruler or other tracking device if they always use one in class when they read.**

✘ **DON'T mark it wrong if the student says either "ell" or "eye" for the symbol *l*.**

Phoneme Segmentation Fluency (Word Segmenting)

What Is It?

Phoneme Segmentation Fluency in Acadience Reading (and similar measures from other publishers) is an indicator of phonemic awareness used for screening in kindergarten and first grade, and for progress monitoring older struggling readers. As with First Sound Fluency, you read a list of words one at a time, but ask students to identify and produce all of the sounds (phonemes) in each word. It is typically a one-minute timed task.

Why Assess It?

The ability to segment the sounds of oral language is another indicator of phonemic awareness (a higher-level skill than identifying just the first sound in a word in FSF), and a strong predictor of future reading success.

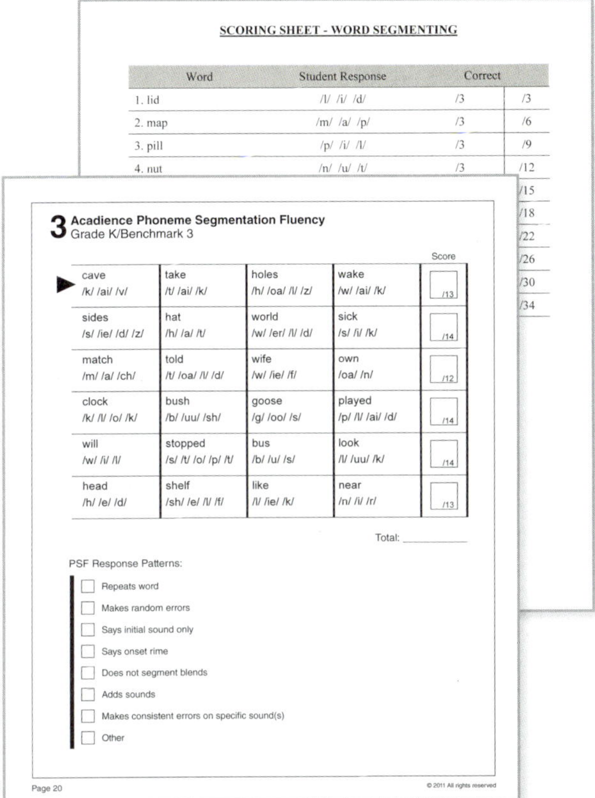

SCORING SHEET - WORD SEGMENTING

Word	Student Response	Correct	
1. lid	/l/ /i/ /d/	/3	/3
2. map	/m/ /a/ /p/	/3	/6
3. pill	/p/ /i/ /l/	/3	/9
4. nut	/n/ /u/ /t/	/3	/12
			/15
			/18
			/22
			/26
			/30
			/34

3 Acadience Phoneme Segmentation Fluency
Grade K/Benchmark 3

				Score
cave /k/ /ai/ /v/	take /t/ /ai/ /k/	holes /h/ /oa/ /l/ /z/	wake /w/ /ai/ /k/	/13
sides /s/ /ie/ /d/ /z/	hat /h/ /a/ /t/	world /w/ /er/ /l/ /d/	sick /s/ /i/ /k/	/14
match /m/ /a/ /ch/	told /t/ /oa/ /l/ /d/	wife /w/ /ie/ /f/	own /oa/ /n/	/12
clock /k/ /l/ /o/ /k/	bush /b/ /uu/ /sh/	goose /g/ /oo/ /s/	played /p/ /l/ /ai/ /d/	/14
will /w/ /i/ /l/	stopped /s/ /t/ /o/ /p/ /t/	bus /b/ /u/ /s/	look /l/ /uu/ /k/	/14
head /h/ /e/ /d/	shelf /sh/ /e/ /l/ /f/	like /l/ /ie/ /k/	near /n/ /i/ /r/	/13

Total: ______

PSF Response Patterns:

- Repeats word
- Makes random errors
- Says initial sound only
- Says onset rime
- Does not segment blends
- Adds sounds
- Makes consistent errors on specific sound(s)
- Other

Page 20

© 2011 All rights reserved

(left) Phoneme Segmentation Fluency from Acadience; (right) Word Segmenting Scoring Sheet from FastBridge

✔ **DO score on the fly and trust your gut about what you heard, and…**

✘ **DON'T try to audiotape the assessment and agonize over replaying it to be sure you marked the student's response correctly.** Stephanie learned this the hard way, and says that is one weekend she wishes she could get back! There's no rule against this per se, but it's definitely not an efficient use of your time. Practice until you're confident, and then score it as you hear it.

✘ **DON'T be tricked by *X* (the letter, not the social media platform!).** A Teacher Knowledge Survey study conducted by Louisa Moats and Barbara Foorman in 2003 found that educators often struggle to identify the individual phonemes in words accurately, which Kate can relate to. She had been teaching for more than 20 years when she realized that the letter *x* can represent TWO phonemes in English, /k/ and /s/. (But speaking of the other X, Stephanie and Kate are both active on the platform formerly known as Twitter, as well as Instagram and Facebook. Come engage with us!)

Learn more about phoneme segmentation from Stephanie here.

Nonsense Word Fluency

What Is It?

Stephanie calls this the test teachers love to hate, but she just plain loves it! Most of the negativity toward NWF comes from lack of understanding what it is measuring. Asking students to read nonsense words is a common task on many reading assessments. Nonsense words (also called *nonwords* or *pseudowords*) are words that can be decoded but do not have meaning in the language of assessment (e.g., *mip*, *sog*). Using nonwords for assessment allows a true measure of the alphabetic principle since it removes the possibility that the student has seen the word before and is reading it from memory.

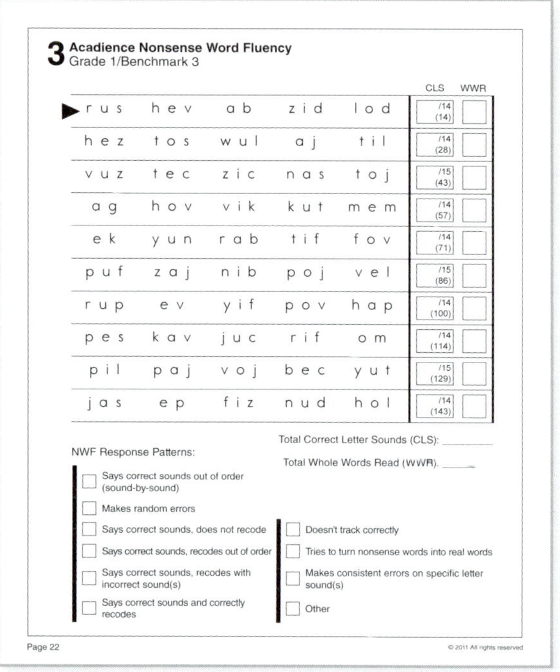

3 Acadience Nonsense Word Fluency
Grade 1/Benchmark 3

					CLS	WWR
▶ r u s	h e v	a b	z i d	l o d	/14 (14)	
h e z	t o s	w u l	a j	t i l	/14 (28)	
v u z	t e c	z i c	n a s	t o j	/15 (43)	
a g	h o v	v i k	k u t	m e m	/14 (57)	
e k	y u n	r a b	t i f	f o v	/14 (71)	
p u f	z a j	n i b	p o j	v e l	/15 (86)	
r u p	e v	y i f	p o v	h a p	/14 (100)	
p e s	k a v	j u c	r i f	o m	/14 (114)	
p i l	p a j	v o j	b e c	y u t	/15 (129)	
j a s	e p	f i z	n u d	h o l	/14 (143)	

Total Correct Letter Sounds (CLS): _______

Total Whole Words Read (WWR): _______

NWF Response Patterns:

- ☐ Says correct sounds out of order (sound-by-sound)
- ☐ Makes random errors
- ☐ Says correct sounds, does not recode
- ☐ Says correct sounds, recodes out of order
- ☐ Says correct sounds, recodes with incorrect sound(s)
- ☐ Says correct sounds and correctly recodes
- ☐ Doesn't track correctly
- ☐ Tries to turn nonsense words into real words
- ☐ Makes consistent errors on specific letter sound(s)
- ☐ Other

Page 22

Nonsense Word Fluency from Acadience

Nonsense Word Fluency in Acadience Reading is used for screening in kindergarten through the beginning of second grade and for progress monitoring older struggling readers. Other publishers have similar nonword reading measures that may assess patterns other than VC and CVC and are used for screening past second grade.

Why Assess It?

- NWF taps into the knowledge of the alphabetic principle (understanding that letters represent the sounds of spoken language) and basic phonics (knowing which letters represent which sounds and being able to blend them into words).
- We can assume nonsense words are brand-new to the student, making them valuable for assessment. If real words are used, the student may read them from memory and the test wouldn't measure the student's knowledge of the alphabetic principle.

- We can also observe if the students can blend automatically or if they still need to sound out each letter before blending. That's a lot to glean from a one-minute task!

TIPS

✔ **DO note response patterns as best you can.** The first few times you conduct any assessment, focusing on accurate timing and administration may be all you can handle, and that's okay! Once you get more comfortable, it can be valuable to use the "response patterns" box (if your screener has one) or simply note something that the child is—or isn't—doing. While some patterns can be seen even if you go back and look at the scoring after the fact (e.g., "Says correct sounds, does not recode"), others need to be noticed in the moment (e.g., "Doesn't track correctly").

✔ **DO read the list of words out loud to yourself before you give it to students for the first time.** It can be helpful to hear yourself speaking the words before you listen to the students read them.

✘ **DON'T give students the benefit of the doubt in scoring.** If you aren't sure if they said the whole word or just said the sounds slowly, score it as if it was just sounds. It is better to identify a student as needing support and quickly learn that he or she doesn't, rather than passing up a student because you were a lenient marker when the student really does need support.

However…

✔ **DO give credit for saying all sounds if students have been taught to sing their sounds when they segment.** For example, "ssssssaaaaaannnnnn" gets full credit for three sounds.

Word Reading Fluency

What Is It?

Word Reading Fluency in DIBELS 8th Edition, aimswebPlus, and easyCBM is an indicator of accuracy and fluency in reading a list of regular and irregular words. It is used for screening in kindergarten through third grade. Students are asked to read as many real words as they can, usually in one minute. These may be words that are decodable to students based on a phonics scope and sequence for their grade or words with unlearned or "irregular" patterns. Typically the list includes high-frequency words.

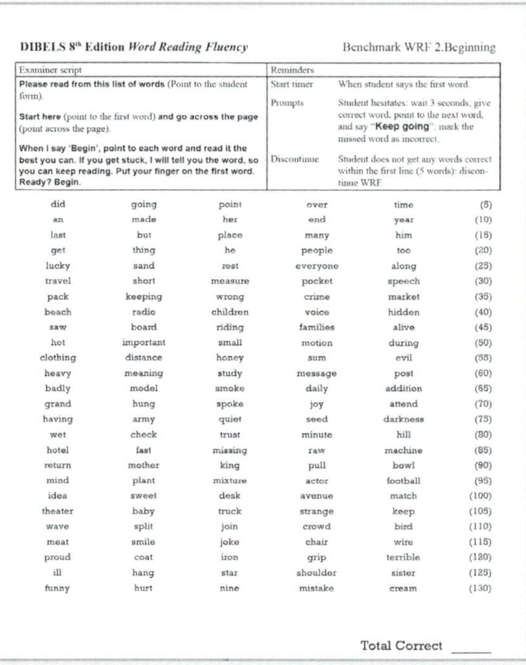

DIBELS 8th Edition *Word Reading Fluency* Benchmark WRF 2.Beginning

Examiner script	Reminders	
Please read from this list of words (Point to the student form). **Start here** (point to the first word) **and go across the page** (point across the page). **When I say 'Begin', point to each word and read it the best you can. If you get stuck, I will tell you the word, so you can keep reading. Put your finger on the first word. Ready? Begin.**	Start timer	When student says the first word.
	Prompts	Student hesitates: wait 3 seconds; give correct word; point to the next word, and say "**Keep going**"; mark the missed word as incorrect.
	Discontinue	Student does not get any words correct within the first line (5 words): discontinue WRF.

did	going	point	over	time	(5)
an	made	her	end	year	(10)
last	but	place	many	him	(15)
get	thing	he	people	too	(20)
lucky	sand	rest	everyone	along	(25)
travel	short	measure	pocket	speech	(30)
pack	keeping	wrong	crime	market	(35)
beach	radio	children	voice	hidden	(40)
saw	board	riding	families	alive	(45)
hot	important	small	motion	during	(50)
clothing	distance	honey	sum	evil	(55)
heavy	meaning	study	message	post	(60)
badly	model	smoke	daily	addition	(65)
grand	hung	spoke	joy	attend	(70)
having	army	quiet	seed	darkness	(75)
wet	check	trust	minute	hill	(80)
hotel	fast	missing	raw	machine	(85)
return	mother	king	pull	bowl	(90)
mind	plant	mixture	actor	football	(95)
idea	sweet	desk	avenue	match	(100)
theater	baby	truck	strange	keep	(105)
wave	split	join	crowd	bird	(110)
meat	smile	joke	chair	wire	(115)
proud	coat	iron	grip	terrible	(120)
ill	hang	star	shoulder	sister	(125)
funny	hurt	nine	mistake	cream	(130)

Total Correct _____

DIBELS 8, University of Oregon

Why Assess It?

Word reading can be a predictor of future reading risk.

✗ **DON'T teach or have students practice the words they'll encounter on the Word Reading Fluency assessment in advance of taking the test.** That would invalidate your results.

Oral Reading Fluency (CBM Reading, Passage Reading Fluency)

What Is It?

Oral Reading Fluency is where Curriculum-Based Measurement began. It is an indicator of reading comprehension, accurate decoding, and text-reading fluency. It is used for screening in first through eighth grade. You ask students to read a passage of connected text for one minute, then calculate scores for accuracy (percentage) and rate (words correct per minute), two of the three elements of reading fluency. (The third element is prosody, or expression, which is not directly measured on this assessment, but on diagnostic assessments of language comprehension, as explained in Chapter 5.)

You may ask students to read three passages (e.g., if using Acadience), using the median score as the data point. Some screeners also include a retell component to ORF, and scores may be given for number of words in the retell and the quality of the retell. While this book focuses on younger grades, we have used Oral Reading Fluency all the way through eighth grade as a valuable tool.

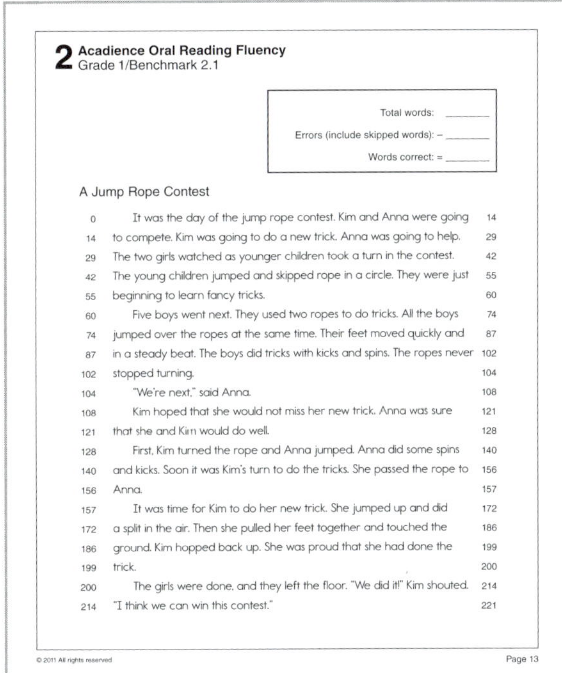

2 **Acadience Oral Reading Fluency**
Grade 1/Benchmark 2.1

Total words: ________
Errors (include skipped words): – ________
Words correct: = ________

A Jump Rope Contest

0 It was the day of the jump rope contest. Kim and Anna were going 14
14 to compete. Kim was going to do a new trick. Anna was going to help. 29
29 The two girls watched as younger children took a turn in the contest. 42
42 The young children jumped and skipped rope in a circle. They were just 55
55 beginning to learn fancy tricks. 60
60 Five boys went next. They used two ropes to do tricks. All the boys 74
74 jumped over the ropes at the same time. Their feet moved quickly and 87
87 in a steady beat. The boys did tricks with kicks and spins. The ropes never 102
102 stopped turning. 104
104 "We're next," said Anna. 108
108 Kim hoped that she would not miss her new trick. Anna was sure 121
121 that she and Kim would do well. 128
128 First, Kim turned the rope and Anna jumped. Anna did some spins 140
140 and kicks. Soon it was Kim's turn to do the tricks. She passed the rope to 156
156 Anna. 157
157 It was time for Kim to do her new trick. She jumped up and did 172
172 a split in the air. Then she pulled her feet together and touched the 186
186 ground. Kim hopped back up. She was proud that she had done the 199
199 trick. 200
200 The girls were done, and they left the floor. "We did it!" Kim shouted. 214
214 "I think we can win this contest." 221

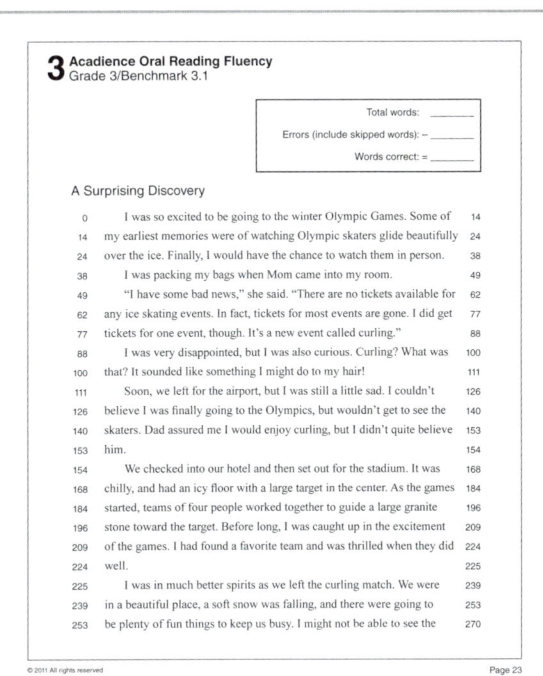

3 **Acadience Oral Reading Fluency**
Grade 3/Benchmark 3.1

Total words: ________
Errors (include skipped words): – ________
Words correct: = ________

A Surprising Discovery

0 I was so excited to be going to the winter Olympic Games. Some of 14
14 my earliest memories were of watching Olympic skaters glide beautifully 24
24 over the ice. Finally, I would have the chance to watch them in person. 38
38 I was packing my bags when Mom came into my room. 49
49 "I have some bad news," she said. "There are no tickets available for 62
62 any ice skating events. In fact, tickets for most events are gone. I did get 77
77 tickets for one event, though. It's a new event called curling." 88
88 I was very disappointed, but I was also curious. Curling? What was 100
100 that? It sounded like something I might do to my hair! 111
111 Soon, we left for the airport, but I was still a little sad. I couldn't 126
126 believe I was finally going to the Olympics, but wouldn't get to see the 140
140 skaters. Dad assured me I would enjoy curling, but I didn't quite believe 153
153 him. 154
154 We checked into our hotel and then set out for the stadium. It was 168
168 chilly, and had an icy floor with a large target in the center. As the games 184
184 started, teams of four people worked together to guide a large granite 196
196 stone toward the target. Before long, I was caught up in the excitement 209
209 of the games. I had found a favorite team and was thrilled when they did 224
224 well. 225
225 I was in much better spirits as we left the curling match. We were 239
239 in a beautiful place, a soft snow was falling, and there were going to 253
253 be plenty of fun things to keep us busy. I might not be able to see the 270

(left) ORF: Grade 1, Benchmark 2.1; (right) ORF: Grade 3, Benchmark 3.1 from Acadience

Why Assess It?

- ORF is an indicator of advanced decoding, reading fluency, and reading comprehension, with the accuracy score providing information about students' phonics and word attack skills.
- Some educators are, at first, uncomfortable with the idea of measuring rate, as this isn't something we did with previous connected text reading assessments. While accuracy needs to come first, there is a strong relationship between words correct per minute and comprehension (more on that in a moment).

- If a retell is part of the assessment, the score provides an additional indicator of comprehension for students who are accurate and fluent readers.

✔ **DO read the passages yourself first.** If your ORF screener includes a retell, read the passage yourself prior to the first assessment so you know what to listen for in the student's retell. Once you've given the same passage multiple times, you'll probably have it memorized, but the first couple of times, especially if you're new to following along and scoring the oral reading, you won't even process the content.

Kate learned this the hard way when a third-grade child began his retell—and she had no idea whether he was providing information from the text or just making up some really believable details about the history of pizza. (She learned afterward that it was the latter!) She had been so focused on scoring his oral reading that she didn't pay attention to the meaning herself—so she made sure not to call the next student until she had read through the passages!

✘ **DON'T read the title to students or ask them to read it.** It's there so you can quickly make sure the correct passage is in front of the student and to make the assessment more like an authentic reading task. This isn't like some past assessments where we would read the title to the student, and perhaps even a description of the text, which might alert them to key vocabulary words.

Kate remembers asking her kindergarten students to read a patterned book where every page ended with "...on the table," and emphasizing the publisher-provided description beforehand: "This story is about a little girl putting her toys ON THE TABLE" with the hopes that it would help them with the word that would not be decodable for them: *table*!

✘ **DON'T be thrown off by the length or difficulty of ORF passages.** We've heard many first-grade teachers in particular express concern over the difficulty of the first ORF passage: "My students will never be able to read this!" The idea is not that students should be able to read the entire passage, or even that they read a portion of it with 100 percent accuracy (which is why ORF screener passages are not designed to be fully decodable based on any phonics scope and sequence).

The passage is being used as a means of assessing their risk level. As an example, a student attempting his or her first Acadience ORF passage in the middle of first grade only needs to read 23 words correct per minute, with an accuracy of 78 percent, to meet the benchmark. See the graphic on page 71, which helps to illustrate that point. Strike-throughs show errors and omissions; the square brackets indicate how far the student read.

Most ORF publishers include a three-second rule, which means if the student hesitates for that long you can provide him or her with the word. You can also watch for students who are in fact able to read phonics patterns that haven't been taught yet, and potentially accelerate where they are in your scope and sequence.

Are You Wondering How All This Connects to Comprehension?

If so, we get it! As noted earlier, research shows that the words correct per minute score is highly correlated with comprehension, and can give us valuable information as a "temperature check."

Reading the words correctly is absolutely necessary, but not enough. The WCPM data helps inform our next steps, as students who are accurate and fluent are ready to take advantage of deeper reading instruction. Students who aren't both accurate and automatic with reading aren't likely to understand the connected text that they read, because their attention is still focused on recognizing words as they decode.

Let's look at a study that Kate shares when she leads screener training, which tends to blow people's minds. In 2001, Fuchs and colleagues measured the correlation between a more formal reading comprehension assessment and shorter measures that could be delivered by classroom teachers.

A perfect correlation would be 1.0, and you can see the following results in the chart at right:

- Clearly there is value in a retell, as it correlates 0.70 with comprehension.
- A cloze (fill-in-the-blanks) assessment correlates slightly higher at 0.72

Above

A Jump Rope Contest

▶ It was the day of the jump rope contest. Kim and Anna were going to compete. Kim was going to do a new trick. Anna was going to help. The two girls watched as younger children took a turn in the contest.

At benchmark

A Jump Rope Contest

▶ It was the day of the jump rope contest. Kim and Anna were going to compete. Kim was going to do a new trick. Anna was going to help.] The two girls watched as younger children took a turn in the contest.

Below benchmark

A Jump Rope Contest

▶ It was the day of the jump rope contest. Kim and Anna were going to compete. Kim was going to do a new trick.] Anna was going to help. The two girls watched as younger children took a turn in the contest.

Well below benchmark

A Jump Rope Contest

▶ It was the day of the jump rope contest. Kim and Anna were going to compete.] Kim was going to do a new trick. Anna was going to help. The two girls watched as younger children took a turn in the contest.

Oral Reading Fluency from Acadience

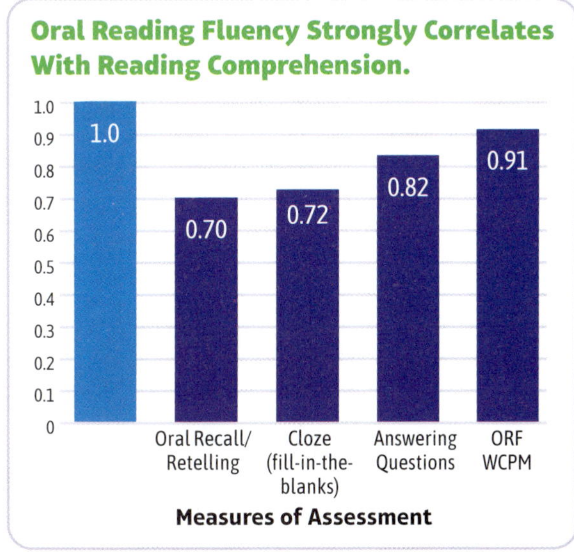

- Having students answer specific questions about a text usually has a lot of social validity for teachers (many educators believe this to be the best way to gauge comprehension), and the study did show that it correlates well at 0.82... but it didn't get the highest score. You may even have encountered students with lots of background knowledge on a topic who can correctly answer the questions at the end of a related passage without even reading it!
- Believe it or not, the words correct per minute score from an Oral Reading Fluency passage actually correlated 0.91 with the students' formal reading comprehension scores! As we mentioned earlier, when students are reading with accuracy and automaticity (at an appropriate rate) their cognitive resources are freed up to actually pay attention to the meaning of what they read.

That said, for some students (approximately one out of 10), ORF scores and scores on other reading comprehension assessments do not correlate. Sometimes those students are multilingual learners, or students on the autism spectrum, who may be able to read accurately, and even at an appropriate rate, without fully understanding the text due to lack of vocabulary or other issues. So continue to watch out for those students, as they may need a different kind of support, even if they meet benchmarks for accuracy and rate. If your ORF includes retell, that will provide you with some additional information.

As Burns and Parker (2014) say in *Curriculum-Based Assessment for Instructional Design*, "When we consult with teachers about students with reading difficulties, we frequently hear that the student 'does not understand a word that he reads.' However, we have discovered that the reason he does not understand a word is that he is not reading the words.... The comprehension deficit is really just a fluency deficit in disguise."

Many reading comprehension difficulties trace back to phonics or even phonemic awareness, so educators should use appropriate diagnostic assessments to

Screening for Risk of Developmental Language Disorder (DLD)

As the Simple View of Reading tells us, language comprehension is an essential factor for successful reading, and students with DLD can have difficulty producing and/or understanding spoken language. Quality screeners for DLD, particularly ones that are accessible to classroom teachers, are not yet in widespread usage, and Bao and colleagues (2024) note that because of this, "nearly half of children with DLD who develop adequate word reading skills are likely to be missed during literacy screening." Bao et al. conducted a study which evaluated 15 commercially available screeners for DLD, and while not all met the traditional criteria for test psychometrics (e.g., reliability, validity), the researchers' focus was to identify screeners that were accurate in their classification of DLD. They share their findings, including recommendations of certain screeners for specific scenarios, in the open-access article "A Review of Screeners to Identify Risk of Developmental Language Disorder."

pinpoint the area of need. You'll find more on choosing diagnostics in Chapter 6, and using data in Chapter 8.

That said, there will also be students who are genuinely challenged in the area of language comprehension (by itself or along with the word recognition component of the Simple View of Reading), which is something that we will see reflected not just in an assessment like this but also in Tier 1 reading instruction and peer and teacher conversations. These students may be identified with Developmental Language Disorder (DLD). Their pattern on screening might be okay on ORF accuracy and words correct but not on retell. Prosody issues (pacing, expression, phrasing) may often be evident as well. But often, what teachers believe to be a "comprehension problem" can be addressed by moving backward through the required skills to find the gap.

Maze

What Is It?

Maze is an indicator of silent reading comprehension that is used for screening in second or third grade (depending on the publisher) through eighth grade. You ask students to read a text passage silently, usually for three minutes. Approximately every seventh word in the passage is deleted, and the student has to choose between three provided possibilities and circle the correct word that makes sense in the sentence; for example, "After school, he [*table, walked, gave*] home." On Acadience and DIBELS 8 Maze, the final score reflects the number of words correct, adjusted for the number of words incorrect, to compensate for possible guessing. Maze can be given individually, to a group, or to a whole class all at the same time. The time for testing is minimal, but scoring the forms afterward takes time, unless students take the assessment on a computer.

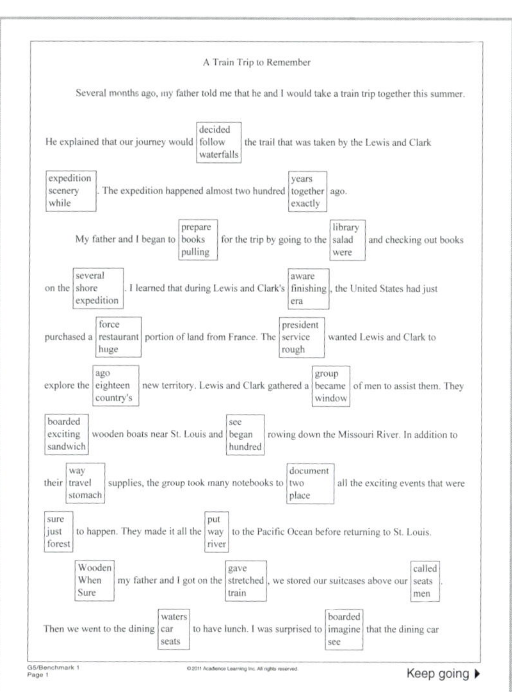

A Train Trip to Remember

Several months ago, my father told me that he and I would take a train trip together this summer.

He explained that our journey would [decided / follow / waterfalls] the trail that was taken by the Lewis and Clark [expedition / scenery / while]. The expedition happened almost two hundred [years / together / exactly] ago.

My father and I began to [prepare / books / pulling] for the trip by going to the [library / salad / were] and checking out books on the [several / shore / expedition]. I learned that during Lewis and Clark's [aware / finishing / era], the United States had just purchased a [force / restaurant / huge] portion of land from France. The [president / service / rough] wanted Lewis and Clark to explore the [ago / eighteen / country's] new territory. Lewis and Clark gathered a [group / became / window] of men to assist them. They [boarded / exciting / sandwich] wooden boats near St. Louis and [see / began / hundred] rowing down the Missouri River. In addition to their [way / travel / stomach] supplies, the group took many notebooks to [document / two / place] all the exciting events that were [sure / just / forest] to happen. They made it all the [put / way / river] to the Pacific Ocean before returning to St. Louis.

[Wooden / When / Sure] my father and I got on the [gave / stretched / train], we stored our suitcases above our [called / seats / men].

Then we went to the dining [waters / car / seats] to have lunch. I was surprised to [boarded / imagine / see] that the dining car

G5/Benchmark 1
Page 1

©2011 Acadience Learning Inc. All rights reserved.

Keep going ▸

Maze: Grade 5, Benchmark 1 from Acadience

Why Assess It?

- Maze provides an indicator of silent reading comprehension, to complement the data gathered from the Oral Reading Fluency measure (as we outlined in the ORF section, words correct per minute and retell are both indicators of comprehension).

✔ **DO use ORF as your primary screener for comprehension, and Maze as a bonus.** With more than 40 years of research supporting the correlation between words correct per minute and comprehension, ORF is our best starting place. Maze provides an additional piece of information for students who are accurate and fluent readers.

Other Screening Measures

There are other screening measures that aren't necessary to use with all students but could be useful in certain contexts, some that are used in grades outside the scope of this book where universal screening might be useful, and some we don't recommend using.

Acadience® Spelling
Word List and Scoring Key
Grade 2 Beginning-of-Year
Form 1

Number	Time	Word and Sentence	Scoring	CSS [cumulative]
1	(start)	**Starfish.** I touched a **starfish. Starfish.**	^s^t^a^r^f^i^s^h^	9 [9]
2	0:10	**Bonnet.** I wore a **bonnet. Bonnet.**	^b^o^n^n^e^t^	7 [16]
3	0:20	**Smiled.** The baby **smiled** at me. **Smiled.**	^s^m^i^l^e^d^	7 [23]
4	0:30	**Fixed. I fixed** my bike. **Fixed.**	^f^i^x^e^d^	6 [29]
5	0:40	**Shiny.** The star is **shiny. Shiny.**	^s^h^i^n^y^	6 [35]
6	0:50	**Birthday.** Happy **birthday** to you. **Birth-day.**	^b^i^r^t^h^d^a^y^	9 [44]
7	1:00	**Cold.** I feel **cold. Cold.**	^c^o^l^d^	5 [49]
8	1:10	**Volunteer.** I'll **volunteer** to help. **Volun-teer.**	^v^o^l^u^n^t^e^e^r^	10 [59]
9	1:20	**Locked.** The door is **locked. Locked.**	^l^o^c^k^e^d^	7 [66]
10	1:30	**Icy.** The street is **icy. Icy.**	^i^c^y^	4 [70]
11	1:40	**Baked.** He **baked** a pie. **Baked.**	^b^a^k^e^d^	6 [76]
12	1:50	**Ponies.** The **ponies** ran. **Ponies.**	^p^o^n^i^e^s^	7 [83]
	2:00	***Stop. Put your pencils down.***		
			Total CSW Possible	12
			Total CSS Possible	83

Spelling Word List and Scoring Key, Grade 2 from Acadience

Spelling

Acadience Spelling is an optional indicator of accurate and fluent spelling that can be used for screening in kindergarten through third grade. Because the research on this measure is ongoing, it is not currently part of the Acadience Reading suite for universal screening. The assessor dictates a list of words for the student to spell, and gives points for Correct Spelling Sequences (CSS) and Correctly Spelled Words (CSW). A spelling screener is typically a timed task (e.g., for two minutes).

Screening English Learners and Speakers of Language Variations

The skills that predict reading proficiency and risk are the same for English learners (ELs) and monolingual students, and explicit, systematic instruction is just as beneficial for them. You can also rest assured that the CIC laid out in this book is applicable to ELs and speakers of language variations, who also benefit from the screening, diagnostic, progress monitoring and outcomes assessments that we describe. When the language of instruction is English, assessment data in English is one key piece of the puzzle.

That said, when assessing students who are ELs, it's a "yes, and…" situation. Yes to following the steps we've laid out, **and** also keeping in mind that we may need to dig deeper into our guiding questions, and tweak our instruction accordingly. For example, we can consider…

Are the errors due to differences between English and the student's home language? While we don't penalize students for errors due to dialect or articulation, scoring correctly requires knowing your students. Researcher and EL expert Elsa Cárdenas-Hagan (personal communication, April 18, 2025) tells us, "a common error pattern is that students do approximations when they get to a sound that doesn't exist in their home language, substituting the closest thing that exists to it"; for example, a Spanish-speaking student saying "sh" as "ch" (when orally isolating/segmenting phonemes or reading words) because "sh" doesn't exist in Spanish. How can you find out what sounds are the same or different between English and a student's home language? The mylanguages.org website is a great resource with information and lessons on almost 100 languages, and AI can be helpful for this too. We tried the sample prompt, "What sounds of spoken language are common to both English and [name of language]? What sounds are unique to each of those languages?" and the site provided lists and examples that can help alert you to potential confusions.

Can we screen in the student's home language? In an ideal world, we would also screen using measures in the student's home language for a more robust picture, as "[t]here is an emerging consensus that measuring bilingual children in both of their languages improves diagnostic accuracy" (Carta & Young, 2019). This makes sense, but of course presents challenges: Is there a scientifically validated tool available in the child's home language? Can we find someone who speaks that language to administer and score it? Fortunately, such tools are available in Spanish, which helps to support the 75 percent of emergent bilinguals in the United States who speak that language at home, such as Acadience Reading Espanol and mCLASS Lectura, and Acadience also has versions in French and Hebrew.

Has the student received English instruction? Just as Kate does not overreact to beginning-of-year screening data for her preK students just entering school, we also want to be cautious with data we get from assessing ELs as they begin English instruction. It's valuable to have as a baseline, and we should respond (with quality instruction and progress monitoring as necessary) but not jump to conclusions (e.g., *This child must have dyslexia*). Further information that comes after the child has received instruction will add to the decision-making process. We always want to be sure that a perceived difficulty is not just due to not yet being taught… and if it is, we must provide the instruction necessary to fill the gaps for that student.

While this book is focused on the assessment of reading and not writing, early spelling ability is actually predictive of future reading risk, especially in kindergarten. And in upper grades, students' reading and spelling skills may not progress together in sequence, making spelling assessment useful. Some states require a spelling assessment for universal screening. For these reasons, we see value in possibly using the spelling assessment with all students if it is useful to answer a Gap Identification or Gap Analysis question for a student or all students in a grade.

TIPS

- ✔ **DO give this to your whole class at the same time.**
- ✔ **DO give all words on the list within the two-minute time limit.**
- ✘ **DON'T say anything to the students other than the scripted directions and prompts.**

Rapid Automatized Naming

Rapid Automatized Naming (RAN) is an indicator of how quickly the visual and language systems are working together. RAN involves many of the processes involved in reading, such as eye movement, sustained attention, matching phonology to print, and working memory. While difficulties with RAN don't seem to impact reading as much as phonemic awareness deficiencies, RAN is also a predictor of future reading skills, so the score can be valuable as another piece of risk assessment, particularly at the beginning of kindergarten, when the predictive power is strongest (Gray & Powell-Smith, 2025). Publishers such as Acadience Learning make RAN materials available for universal screening because it is required in some states.

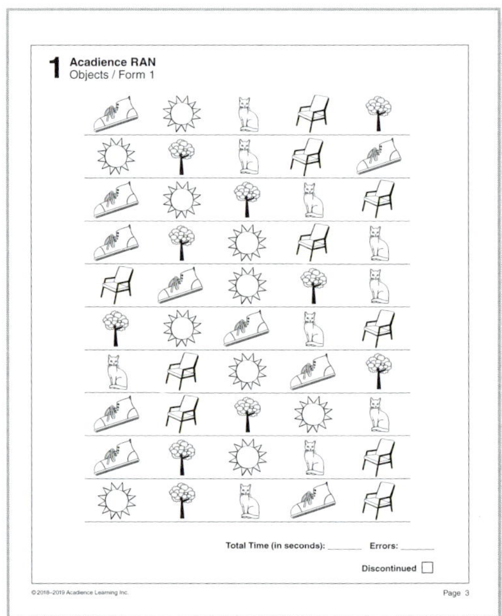

1 Acadience RAN
Objects / Form 1

Total Time (in seconds): ______ Errors: ______

Discontinued ☐

©2018-2019 Acadience Learning Inc.

Page 3

Rapid Automatized Naming from Acadience

Students are asked to name familiar items (e.g., letters, numbers, and/or objects) that are repeated in a grid. Instead of being timed for one minute, the assessor times how long it takes for the student to complete the grid.

TIPS

✔ **DO remember familiarity matters for RAN.** If students can't already name the items on the test, they can't participate in it. In the past, Kate had a couple of students at or above benchmark for phonemic awareness, but still struggling with decoding, and she wanted to see if low RAN might be part of the problem... but she wasn't able to assess them because they didn't know the names of the five letters or five numbers used on the assessment! A RAN task that uses objects may help in this situation.

✘ **DON'T make RAN an instructional goal.** Improving RAN doesn't improve reading outcomes. However, if you teach reading, RAN improves. So the best course of action for students with low RAN is intensifying their evidence-based, explicit instruction, which you should do based on low scores on phonemic awareness and letter naming anyway.

Concepts of Print

Assessment suites such as aimswebPlus and FastBridge include measures of concepts of print. Concepts of print include understanding how books work; knowing the difference between letters, words, and sentences; and recognizing that English print is read from left to right, top to bottom on a page. Because those assessments don't indicate proficiency in essential skill areas, we don't recommend screening all students on concepts of print. But if your state requires it, there are resources available to you.

PreK Screening

It's never too early to start screening and intervening with students! Kate uses the Preschool Early Literacy Indicators (Kaminski et al., 2023) screener from Acadience with her preK students. PELI incorporates a storybook and game format to provide valuable information not just on the early literacy skills that are usually

Is More Information Better?

When it comes to reading assessment, more information is not necessarily better. You don't need, for example, multiple universal screening assessments. If your district uses DIBELS 8th Edition, Acadience Reading, or FastBridge for screening, you don't also need STAR Reading, MAP, or iReady. In fact, different assessments are likely to give you a different picture of the students because they are designed for slightly different purposes, tap into different skills, and measure what students know in different ways. So we recommend you resist the temptation to "triangulate" data.

measured, such as alphabet knowledge and phonological awareness, but also vocabulary/oral language and comprehension. Because this assessment is done at the very start of the students' formal schooling, Kate finds that low scores at the beginning of the year on alphabet knowledge and phonological awareness tend to jump significantly by the middle of the year just with strong Tier 1 instruction, but vocabulary/oral language and comprehension scores can be early red flags of a language concern. We will provide more ideas for assessing language comprehension in Chapter 5.

In Closing, Remember...

Universal screening is key to finding students who are struggling or at risk, and identifying systems that need improvement.

After screening, you need to analyze the data and target instruction for students below benchmark, as well as consider changes to Tier 1 instruction. We've got you covered. Keep reading!

Sometimes, screening gives you all the information you need to start teaching.

Often, though, we need more data to make instructional decisions, and in Chapter 5, we walk you through the process of diagnostic assessment so you can figure out what exactly to teach your students next.

Chapter 6 details how to monitor the progress of students who are receiving targeted intervention, Chapter 7 explains outcome assessment, and Chapter 8 digs further into pulling all of this together to use assessment data within your classroom and school!

Diagnostic Assessment
What Should Be Taught and How?

CHAPTER 5

Your screening is done. Yes! But now what? We don't collect screening data just to categorize students as being on track or not on track, and then file it away. We should use it to inform instruction and improve student achievement. In some cases, screening results are all we need to plan instruction, and in others, when those results don't tell us what to teach next, we need to proceed to a diagnostic assessment. In this chapter, we guide you through that process!

Just as doctors use screening tests and clinical questioning to determine next tests for their patients, educators use screening and questioning to determine diagnostic assessments, if any. If you aren't sure what to teach next, or have lingering questions about your instructional plan, diagnostic assessments will help you make an educated guess or hypothesis about what to change to get better results for your students. In our experience, the most useful diagnostic assessments are ones that link closely to instruction, not norm-referenced tests like the Comprehensive Test of Phonological Processing (CTOPP) or the Wechsler Individual Achievement Test, Fourth Edition (WIAT-4). Even when students are suspected to have a reading disability, we see little use for tests that are not closely connected to instruction. If you are sure what to teach and don't have a question, no further assessment is needed, and you can proceed with instruction and Step 3: Action Planning. See Chapter 8 for details.

DIAGNOSTIC ASSESSMENT

ANALOGY: X-ray
(The screening we've done tells us this student needs more in-depth assessment.)

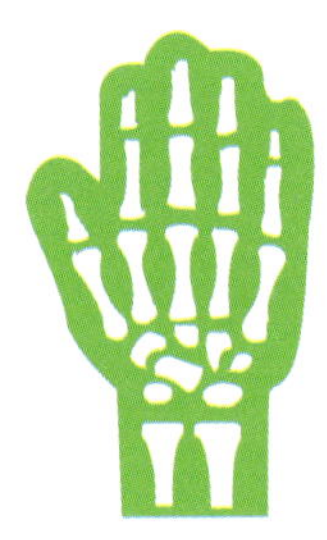

Step	Key Questions	Assessment Purpose
1. Gap Identification	• Which students and systems need help? • What is the gap between actual and desired outcomes?	Universal Screening
2. Gap Analysis	• What should be taught and how? • Why is the gap happening?	Diagnostic Assessment
3. Action Planning	• What is the plan to close the gap?	
4. Outcome Analysis	• Is the instruction working? • Did the instruction work?	Progress Monitoring Outcome Assessment

What Are Characteristics of a Quality Diagnostic Assessment?

How do you spot a quality diagnostic assessment? Look for these characteristics:

- **It is given to specific students (not everyone) to determine what to teach next.** Sometimes screening data is all we need to determine an individual student's learning gap. For example, if the student's First Sound Fluency score is below benchmark, then isolating first sounds is the skill to target. But other times, screening data is not enough to determine a learning gap, and we must therefore give a diagnostic assessment, for example, when a third-grade student scores below benchmark on the accuracy percentage on Oral Reading Fluency.
- **It is more in-depth than screening.** Diagnostic assessments don't just tell us who is at risk, they also provide details about the specific subskills that students need to acquire on a scale from easy to more challenging.
- **It may or may not be given under standardized testing conditions, the way screeners are.** Because the purpose of a diagnostic assessment is to get to the bottom of what to teach next, comparing students to others or to a benchmark score is not important. Therefore, standardized testing conditions are not necessary. Diagnostic assessments don't necessarily have to be timed. Some encourage standardized directions and

prompts, but allow lots of flexibility in administering the assessment, such as rewording the question, using manipulatives, and providing scaffolds. The goal is to find what to teach and how much support the student needs to learn it.

- **It is closely linked to instruction.** Diagnostic assessments should tell you what to teach tomorrow. The score on a diagnostic (e.g., 35 points) is far less important than the reason for the score (e.g., the student sounded out words with short vowels and consonants but started making errors on words with long vowels).

Good screeners are usually not good diagnostics because the two types of assessments answer completely different questions. As Stephanie likes to say, screening puts you in the ballpark of a student's needs, whereas a diagnostic assessment gives you the row and seat numbers!

Examples of Diagnostic Assessments

- Acadience Reading Diagnostic
  - Phonemic Awareness and Word Reading and Decoding (PA & WRD)
  - Comprehension, Fluency and Oral Language (CFOL)
- Really Great Reading (Beginning Decoding Survey, Advanced Decoding Survey)
- Quick Phonics Screener*
- CORE Phonics Survey
- 95 Percent Group's Phonics Screener for Intervention*
- University of Florida Literacy Institute (UFLI) Foundations Intervention Placement Test
- Spelling inventories
- Informal assessments of syntax, vocabulary, and morphology

*These tools meet our definition of diagnostics, despite what their names indicate.

Choosing a Diagnostic Assessment

The Simple View of Reading tells us that reading comprehension is the product of word recognition and language comprehension, so using it as a schema can help us choose an assessment: If a student can't decode, we need a diagnostic to dig into that. If she or he can't understand language, we need a language comprehension diagnostic—and it's possible the student could need both.

Next, we offer a variety of scenarios to help you pinpoint skills that may need to be assessed more deeply, based on screening results.

Digging Into Decoding

Scenario 1: Student does not reach benchmark for phonemic awareness (e.g., First Sound Fluency, Initial Sounds, Onset Sounds, Phoneme Segmentation Fluency, Word Segmenting)	Do we know what to teach next?	Do we need a diagnostic?
	Yes—phonemic awareness	No

This pattern indicates that the student might need help learning phonemic awareness skills such as isolating, blending, and segmenting phonemes.

As we mentioned earlier, if a student does not meet the benchmark goal for segmenting phonemes on screening, then that's the skill you need to target. Typically, students can first isolate the beginning sound in a Consonant-Vowel-Consonant (CVC) word, then the final sound, and finally the medial (middle) sound, so that's a good order to follow in terms of instruction and intervention.

Some diagnostic assessments begin with the larger units of phonological sensitivity, such as syllable and rhyme awareness, which we know are not necessary to teach for most students to learn to read (Brady, 2020; International Dyslexia Association, 2022; National Institute of Child Health and Human Development, 2000), so why waste time?

Diagnostics that look at orally manipulating (adding, deleting, substituting) sounds in a word may not be necessary because those skills are the result of reading and spelling, not the prerequisites for them (Brown et al., 2021; Burgess & Lonigan, 1998; Castles et al., 2011; Clemens et al., 2021; Foulin, 2005; Lerner & Lonigan, 2016). As researcher Susan Brady once explained to Kate, "If we're not going to be teaching these skills, there's no need to assess them. It just causes confusion about what you should attend to."

Scenario 2: Student does not reach benchmark for letter sounds and blending (Nonsense Word Fluency—NWF) but does for phonemic awareness (PSF).	Do we know what to teach next?	Do we need a diagnostic?
	Yes—instruction should include letter sounds and blending.	No

This pattern indicates the student may have phonemic awareness skills but needs to learn letter-sound relationships and how to blend letter sounds into words. If the Acadience Reading NWF assessment was used, no additional diagnostic assessment is necessary, and instruction should focus on connecting phonemes to graphemes and reading (real, not nonsense) basic CVC words, since that is the pattern the student struggled with on screening. If the DIBELS 8th Edition NWF assessment was used, a decoding diagnostic would be useful for determining which phonics patterns to teach next, since that version of NWF includes patterns beyond CVC.

Scenario 3: Student does not reach benchmark for Oral Reading Fluency (ORF) Accuracy but does for NWF

Do we know what to teach next?	Do we need a diagnostic?
No	**Yes—administer a decoding diagnostic**

This pattern indicates the student can read basic phonics patterns but has difficulty reading all the phonics patterns that appear in the ORF passage.

As the Simple View of Reading shows us, being able to accurately read words is essential for reading comprehension. A low accuracy score on a one-minute ORF screening indicates the student is having difficulty with word recognition. But the screening is too brief to pinpoint exactly which phonics patterns the student knows and needs to learn. Is it *r*-controlled vowels? Digraphs? Decoding diagnostics such as Phonics Survey (CORE, 2008), Quick Phonics Screener (Hasbrouck, 2025), and Beginning and Advanced Decoding Surveys (Farrell & Hunter, 2016), as well as Acadience Reading Diagnostic for Word Reading and Decoding (Acadience Learning, 2022), can help us to see where a particular student has a gap and what to teach next.

Occasionally, students won't meet benchmark for NWF, where letter-sound correspondences and blending are required, yet manage to meet benchmark for ORF. When that happens, be concerned, as those students may have memorized whole words and learned strategies to help them compensate when reading connected text, yet they are still missing foundational skills that could help them be more successful readers.

Our favorite decoding diagnostics are placement tests that route students directly into an intervention program, making the decision-making easy for teachers, as we then know exactly where to start with the students in that particular program. The examples that follow are from the Phonics Screener from the 95 Percent Group and the UFLI Foundations Intervention Placement Test.

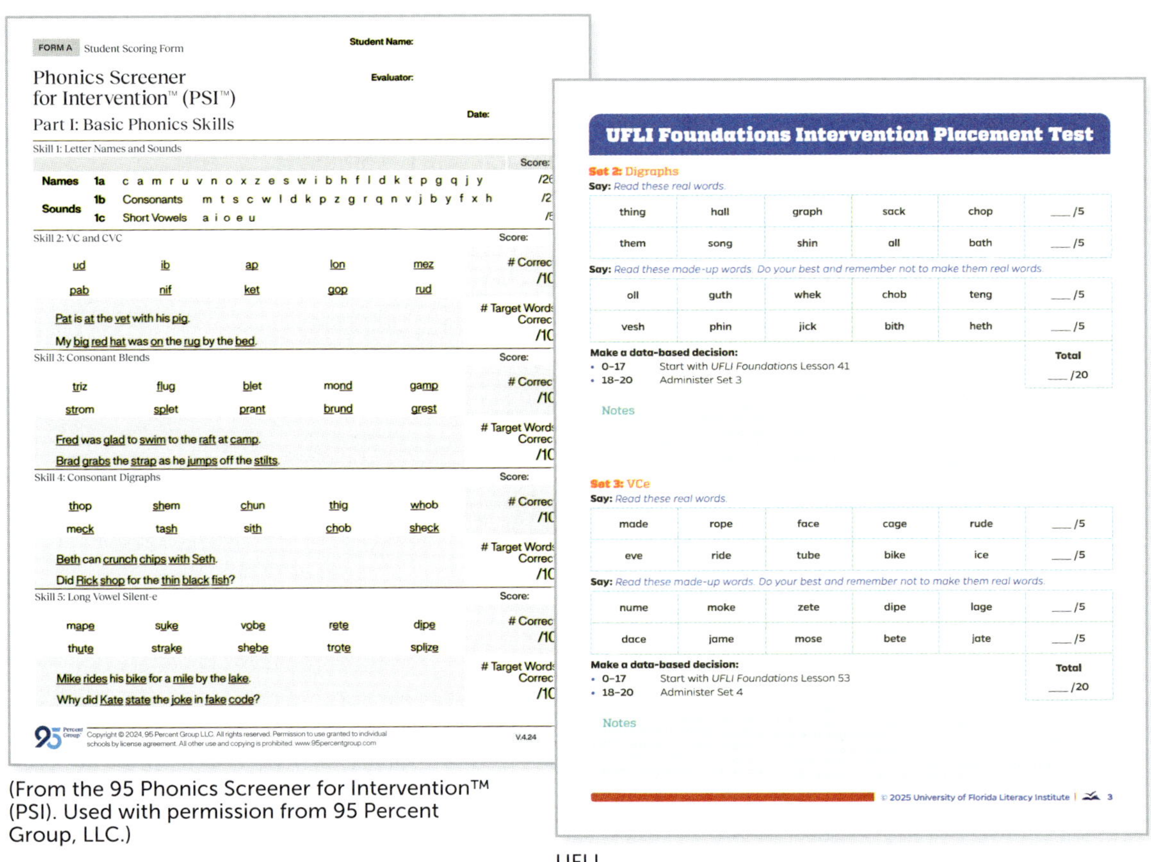

FORM A Student Scoring Form

Student Name:

Evaluator:

Date:

Phonics Screener for Intervention™ (PSI™)

Part I: Basic Phonics Skills

Skill 1: Letter Names and Sounds

				Score:
Names	1a		c a m r u v n o x z e s w i b h f l d k t p g q j y	/26
Sounds	1b	Consonants	m t s c w l d k p z g r q n v j b y f x h	/2
	1c	Short Vowels	a i o e u	/5

Skill 2: VC and CVC

ud ib ap lon mez

pab nif ket gop rud

Pat is at the vet with his pig.

My big red hat was on the rug by the bed.

Score: # Correct /10 # Target Words Correct /10

Skill 3: Consonant Blends

triz flug blet mond gamp

strom splet prant brund grest

Fred was glad to swim to the raft at camp.

Brad grabs the strap as he jumps off the stilts.

Score: # Correct /10 # Target Words Correct /10

Skill 4: Consonant Digraphs

thop shem chun thig whob

meck tash sith chob sheck

Beth can crunch chips with Seth.

Did Rick shop for the thin black fish?

Score: # Correct /10 # Target Words Correct /10

Skill 5: Long Vowel Silent-e

mape suke vobe rete dipe

thute strake shebe trote splize

Mike rides his bike for a mile by the lake.

Why did Kate state the joke in fake code?

Score: # Correct /10 # Target Words Correct /10

 V.4.24

(From the 95 Phonics Screener for Intervention™ (PSI). Used with permission from 95 Percent Group, LLC.)

UFLI Foundations Intervention Placement Test

Set 2: Digraphs

Say: *Read these real words.*

thing	hall	graph	sack	chop	___ /5
them	song	shin	all	bath	___ /5

Say: *Read these made-up words. Do your best and remember not to make them real words.*

oll	guth	whek	chob	teng	___ /5
vesh	phin	jick	bith	heth	___ /5

Make a data-based decision:
- 0–17 Start with *UFLI Foundations* Lesson 41
- 18–20 Administer Set 3

Total ___ /20

Notes

Set 3: VCe

Say: *Read these real words.*

made	rope	face	cage	rude	___ /5
eve	ride	tube	bike	ice	___ /5

Say: *Read these made-up words. Do your best and remember not to make them real words.*

nume	moke	zete	dipe	lage	___ /5
dace	jame	mose	bete	jate	___ /5

Make a data-based decision:
- 0–17 Start with *UFLI Foundations* Lesson 53
- 18–20 Administer Set 4

Total ___ /20

Notes

 3

UFLI

Scenario 4: Student does not reach benchmark for ORF Words Correct Per Minute but does for ORF Accuracy

Do we know what to teach next?	Do we need a diagnostic?
Yes—instruction should focus on automaticity (rate) aspect of fluency	No

This pattern indicates that the student is reading accurately, but not automatically enough to comprehend the text, so instruction should target building fluency.

Digging Into Language Comprehension

Reading comprehension can be tricky to assess. When students in third grade and above score low on screening measures that indicate reading comprehension, teachers and parents may automatically assume that those students have comprehension issues. While it is true the students aren't understanding grade-level text, it is possible their issue is actually related to accuracy and/or rate of decoding, as we talked about in the Oral Reading Fluency section of Chapter 4 on screening. However, if accuracy and rate are where they should be, and reading comprehension is still a concern (which would show up in screening data through ORF Retell and Maze), then language comprehension should be investigated. A school or district speech-language pathologist can also be a huge asset when you're looking into language and reading comprehension concerns.

Scenario 5: Student does not reach benchmark for ORF Retell and/or Maze but does for ORF Accuracy and WCPM

Do we know what to teach next?	Do we need a diagnostic?
No	**Yes—administer a language comprehension diagnostic**

This pattern indicates the student is an accurate and fluent reader but surprisingly is not understanding what she reads.

But which aspects of language comprehension are impairing the student's reading comprehension? To answer that question, we should ask ourselves more precise questions:

- Does the student have adequate listening comprehension?
- Does she have adequate vocabulary knowledge?
- Does she have adequate knowledge of English syntax and morphology?

Listening Comprehension

When one of your students shows difficulty understanding a passage he's read independently, ask yourself if he can understand it when someone reads it to him. To do an informal listening comprehension check, simply read a text aloud to the student, and then ask him comprehension questions to gauge his understanding. This can be particularly beneficial with English learners, as we try to figure out if language comprehension is the barrier to understanding a text, or if it's actually word recognition.

Do We Need to Assess Prosody?

Prosody refers to aspects of speech, such as rhythm, intonation, and stress. It is involved in language processing and interpretation. Many educators believe reading with prosody, or expression, is important, and in fact, many believe it is an essential goal of reading instruction. Research suggests reading with prosody is related to reading comprehension (Kuhn & Stahl, 2000), but it isn't clear if prosody causes comprehension or if comprehension causes prosody (Dowhower, 1991). Therefore, we recommend modeling prosodic reading but only potentially assessing it and targeting it for intervention with the small percentage of students who are accurate and fluent readers but not comprehending. Observing students during oral reading is one way to measure prosody (Hudson, 2005), such as with the Acadience Reading Diagnostic: CFOL. We've provided the Prosody Assessment Rating Scale from CORE below as an example to give you an idea of what the look-fors might be when assessing prosody.

Prosody Assessment Rating Scale

FEATURES OF SPOKEN LANGUAGE	NONPROSODIC			PROSODIC
	LEVEL 1	**LEVEL 2**	**LEVEL 3**	**LEVEL 4**
Stress	Equally stresses each word in a sentence	Equally stresses each word in a sentence or stresses the unimportant words in a sentence	Stresses the most important words in a sentence	Stresses all appropriate words in a sentence
Phrasing	Reads primarily word by word	Reads primarily in two-word phrases, but sometimes word by word	Reads primarily in three-word phrases	Reads primarily in larger, meaningful phrases
	Often pauses after every word and within words	Often pauses within phrases	Often pauses between phrases, but occasionally pauses within them	Consistently pauses at the end of clauses and sentences
	Chunks words with no attention to author's syntax or does not chunk them at all	Chunks words with little attention to author's syntax	Often chunks words appropriately, preserving author's syntax	Consistently chunks words appropriately, preserving author's syntax
Intonation	Does not change pitch to reflect end marks	Occasionally changes pitch to reflect end marks	Often changes pitch to reflect end marks	Consistently changes pitch to reflect end marks
Expression	Reads in a monotone	Occasionally uses voice to reflect character's emotions or actions	Usually uses voice to reflect character's emotions or actions	Consistently uses voice to reflect character's emotions or actions
Pauses	Reads from one sentence to the next without pausing for punctuation	Pauses between sentences only when there is a period	Usually pauses at commas and end marks	Consistently pauses appropriately at all punctuation

(CORE)

Some screeners include listening comprehension measures, such as the Acadience Preschool Early Literacy Indicators (PELI) (Kaminski et al., 2023) and aimswebPlus Listening Comprehension.

Different diagnostic assessments exist to dig deeper into this area as well. Acadience's Reading Diagnostic Tool includes Comprehension, Fluency and Oral Language (CFOL) (Powell-Smith et al., 2021), which contains a listening comprehension measure for which you ask the student to listen to passages and then provide retells and answer questions about what he heard.

Vocabulary and Word Knowledge

In a 2014 study, Spencer and colleagues looked at 425,000 students in first, second, and third grades who had poor reading comprehension and found that only one percent of those students had adequate decoding and vocabulary skills. If decoding is ruled out as an issue for a particular student, it's possible that vocabulary is the issue, particularly for multilingual learners, which makes a vocabulary diagnostic, such as the Acadience CFOL, valuable.

We can measure vocabulary and word knowledge by having students provide definitions, provide two meanings for words with multiple meanings, and/or explain the meaning of specific idioms (phrases or expressions that are typically not meant literally), all of which are included in the Acadience CFOL.

Morphological Awareness

Morphology, which involves understanding how the smallest meaningful parts of words come together, is another contributor to comprehension. (It also plays a role in accurate decoding.) Deb Glaser's *Morphemes for Little Ones* (2023) includes handy "Informal Criterion Morphological Awareness Assessments," which ask students to complete various morphological tasks. For example, when prompted with "The kids were *excited* to go on a field trip. They were filled with...," the target response is "excitement," changing the suffix to take the word from an adjective to a noun.

On the Acadience Reading Diagnostic: CFOL, the Morphological Awareness measures ask students to compound morphemes (put two or more morphemes together to make a word, e.g., *cup* and *cake* to make *cupcake*), complete sentences, and create words with morphemes to assess their morphological awareness.

Syntax

Readers need to understand syntax, or how words and phrases are arranged to make sentences, to comprehend what they read.

Acadience's CFOL measures syntactic knowledge by having students match sentences to pictures, rearrange mixed-up sentences (anagrams), and repeat sentences.

Never Say Never to Using a Diagnostic With All Students

Sometimes administering a diagnostic to all students, like you would a screener, makes sense. For example, in Kate's Ontario kindergarten program, she has students for two years: Year 1 for preK and Year 2 for kindergarten. When preK students return to her after one year of explicit and systematic phonics instruction, she uses a letter-sound assessment to check *which* letter names and corresponding sounds each of them knows. This can be done quite quickly, and she uses the data right away, with targeted instruction, and includes families in helping to fill any letter-sound gaps.

Occasionally, Kate uncovers an instructional issue, such as the year she discovered that two-thirds of the students didn't recognize the uppercase *Q*. When reteaching it, she explained to her students that when so many of them hadn't learned uppercase *Q*, that was a Mrs. Winn problem!

Stephanie finds it helpful to use a spelling assessment in grades 3–6 with an entire class or grade when there is a question about the gap between students' reading and spelling skills. These group-administered assessments offer an efficient indication of fully mapped phonics patterns. Keep in mind that advanced readers, who may be at or above benchmark on reading measures, might still benefit from work on spelling. This is especially the case for older students who may not have had effective phonics instruction that integrated spelling in the early grades. If you can read a word, you can't necessarily spell it, but if you can spell a word, you can read it. As our friend Pam Kastner says, "Teaching spelling is teaching reading."

That said, remember: There's no point in collecting data if you're not going to use it!

Who Should Administer Diagnostic Assessments?

Despite what the name may bring to mind, you don't need a medical degree to use "diagnostic" assessments. Classroom teachers can and should administer them! If a special education teacher or interventionist conducts diagnostic assessments at your school, be sure to discuss the results, especially if you will be the one delivering the targeted instruction.

Survey Level Assessment

Survey Level Assessment (or what Stephanie likes to call "Diagnostic Light") can help teachers find the optimal point for instruction and progress monitoring for students in second grade and above (more on progress monitoring in Chapter 6).

The term "levels" does not refer to a system of leveled books. It refers to skill levels along the path to reading—from phonemic awareness, to phonics, to accurate and fluent reading, to reading comprehension—or levels of materials from an assessment such as Acadience Reading: FSF to PSF to NWF to ORF.

Universal screening involves measuring performance on skills students should master within their assigned grade level. When students don't do well on universal screening, we may need diagnostic assessment to determine exactly what to teach next. Survey Level Assessment functions like a bridge between universal screening and diagnostic assessment by using screening measures strategically to determine where to start diagnostic assessment. It can make diagnostic assessment more targeted and efficient.

Using Survey Level Assessment to Target Instruction

Survey Level Assessment is conducted by working backwards from the screening scores through the skill levels and test materials until you find the level at which the student reaches the benchmark goal. If the student doesn't meet the goal, you keep dropping back. The skill that is just above where the student met the goal is the one to focus on for instruction. For example, if the student meets the goal for segmenting phonemes, basic phonics and blending would be the next instructional targets.

Survey Level Assessment, which involves the Oral Reading Fluency measure, is typically done by giving three passages and using the median words correct and the median errors to calculate the accuracy percent (*median words correct* divided by *median correct plus median errors* multiplied by 100 = accuracy percent), but you could test back using just one passage.

Grade-Level Considerations

Surveying back is typically done with students in second grade and above. It isn't necessary to survey back with students in kindergarten and first grade because all of the measures that you might survey back to have been given during universal screening. However, the thought process is still useful in kindergarten and first grade for determining instructional targets and progress-monitoring level. For example, if a first-grade student doesn't meet the screening goals on ORF, NWF, or PSF, no additional diagnostic assessment is needed; instruction can start with the lowest skills in the sequence: phonemic awareness, letter sounds, and reading basic words, and PSF can be used for progress monitoring.

If you have data on a student from universal screening in past years, use that information to inform where to start instruction. If you know or suspect that the student is reading several grade levels below her assigned grade, jump straight to that grade.

Survey Materials

Materials for Survey Level Assessment are available for free and for purchase.

Materials for Free

Survey Level Assessment can be done with the free progress-monitoring materials for assessments, such as Acadience Reading or DIBELS 8th Edition, which are available online. Copy a set of test materials for each measure and level of ORF. For example, we would use progress-monitoring form 20 for FSF, PSF, and NWF, and passages 18, 19, and 20 for levels 1–6 of ORF. That way, if you end up using one of those assessments for progress monitoring (more about that in Chapter 6), at least 17 weeks will have passed before you get to those forms and, therefore, there won't be any impact from the students previously being exposed to the test materials.

Materials for Purchase

The Acadience Reading Survey (Powell-Smith et al., 2021) can be purchased for a reasonable price, and it contains a manual that describes the process and includes case examples.

Go here for survey-level resources, including case examples and a blank recording form.

The advantages of purchasing the Survey Kit is that it comes with alternate forms of each measure at the same level of difficulty that were created specifically for Survey Level Assessment, research-informed guidelines for testing back, and case examples. The survey forms are carefully constructed to be at the same level of difficulty as the Acadience Reading screening and progress-monitoring forms.

The Instructional Hierarchy: An Additional Tool for Diagnostic Assessment

We introduced the Instructional Hierarchy in Chapter 1 (another "Why wasn't I taught this before?" concept for Kate). Here's a quick recap:

1. Acquisition phase (student reads slowly and inaccurately)
2. Fluency-building phase (student reads accurately, but still slowly)
3. Generalization and adaptation phase (student reads accurately and at a good rate, and can apply those skills to new settings and use them to problem solve)

It is important to consider this hierarchy when determining your next instructional steps, and your assessment data can guide you.

As Amanda VanDerHeyden and Matt Burns (2023) write, "Evidence-based interventions are a good starting place, but the intervention must be selected based on the student's needs. Formative or diagnostic assessment of student learning directs us to interventions with a strong research base that also matches the needs of learners at that moment of instruction." The important question to determine the right intervention is, Are the learners in the acquisition phase or the fluency-building phase?

Diagnostic Assessment for Advanced Readers

Keep in mind, diagnostic assessments aren't only for at-risk learners. Kate recently used the CORE Phonics assessment to determine where to begin differentiated phonics instruction for an advanced reader. The student was beginning kindergarten and, as such, was too young for the school's "gifted" assessment, but was already reading well past the kindergarten scope and sequence. While Kate has found that accurate decoders frequently still benefit from letter formation, fluency, and spelling work using letters and sounds from the kindergarten scope and sequence, this particular student was also ready for more advanced reading instruction, and the diagnostic assessment helped her target where to begin.

Amanda Nickerson, one of Kate's guests on *Reading Road Trip*, completed a study with advanced readers for her doctoral dissertation (her committee was chaired by Stephanie), and used a Survey Level Assessment to "test up" (instead of backwards) to find the best fit for instruction and progress monitoring for her study participants. "Above-level assessments can really guide us and help us identify those next steps for instruction," says Dr. Nickerson, "and that can help us purposefully accelerate students through a scope and sequence or a learning progression that helps us quickly learn the content and go deeper to provide that depth and complexity that students benefit from."

Matt Burns shares a story about a student who began receiving a repeated-reading intervention to improve fluency, targeting his WCPM. While there is extensive research to support repeated reading, the intervention was not successful. Thinking about the instructional hierarchy, the educators in charge decided to switch to an accuracy intervention, focused on increasing the percentage of words he could read correctly, during which the student made a lot of growth. *Then* the educators returned to the fluency intervention, and the student's WCPM began to climb quickly. Accuracy has to be established before you can expect fluency.

Placing a student within the instructional hierarchy is a good way to squeeze "diagnostic-ish" information from brief, direct screening assessments, such as Acadience Reading and DIBELS 8th Edition. Even when students score at or above benchmark on a screening assessment, we can ask ourselves, Is the student accurate and fluent? Answering that question doesn't require doing a diagnostic test; it requires looking at the specific scoring notation on the screening assessment that capture the students' behaviors—see examples below.

Students who read slowly and inaccurately need more instruction in accurate decoding. Students who read accurately but slowly need to practice reading to become fluent. And students who read accurately and fluently should be encouraged to apply their skills to more challenging tasks.

Student Examples

To illustrate the value of determining where students are on the instructional hierarchy, we offer five examples of NWF-CLS scoring forms on the next page, which show students who need very different types of instruction.

The first three examples show students in the acquisition phase of the instructional hierarchy (although the instruction they need varies), the fourth example shows a student in the fluency-building phase, and the last example shows a student in the generalization and adaptation phase.

If you're not familiar with scoring notation for Acadience's NWF measure:

- Single underlined letters indicate the student was decoding sound by sound.
- Single underlined letters with a solid line underneath each word indicate the student decoded sound by sound and then recoded into a word.
- A solid underline beneath a whole word indicates that the student was reading whole words (which is the desired response) without going sound by sound.
- Strike-throughs show the sounds that were errors.

Rose: Acquisition Phase

Rose is making errors while reading individual letter sounds. She needs to learn to match sounds to letters correctly and to blend letters to read words.

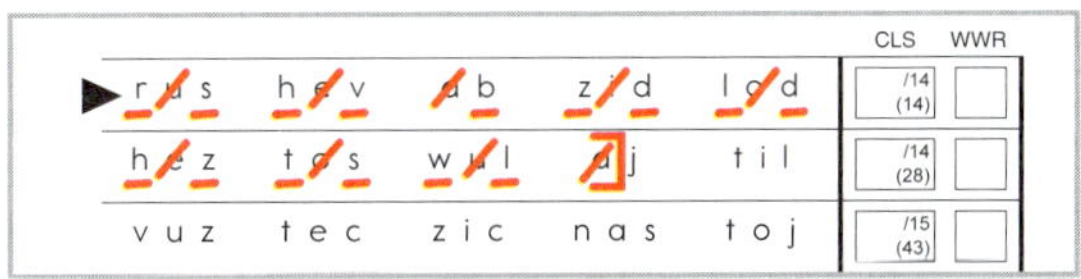

					CLS	WWR
r u s	h e v	a b	z i d	l o d	/14 (14)	
h e z	t o s	w u l	a j	t i l	/14 (28)	
v u z	t e c	z i c	n a s	t o j	/15 (43)	

Peter: Acquisition Phase

Peter is making errors on letter sounds while reading whole words. He's not going sound by sound, but is still making the same number of errors as Rose.

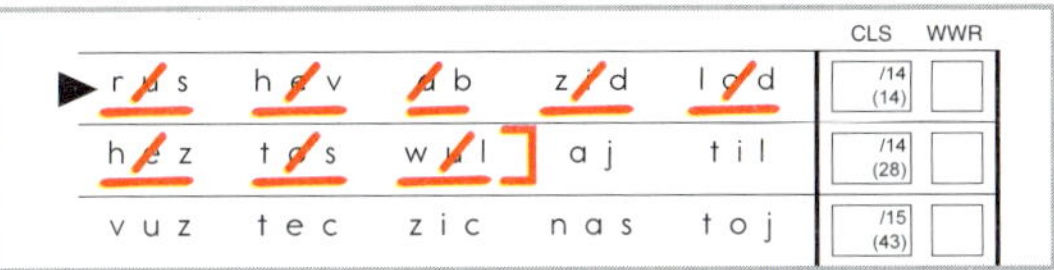

					CLS	WWR
r u s	h e v	a b	z i d	l o d	/14 (14)	
h e z	t o s	w u l	a j	t i l	/14 (28)	
v u z	t e c	z i c	n a s	t o j	/15 (43)	

Mira: Acquisition Phase

Mira can read letter sounds accurately and needs to learn to blend letter sounds to read words.

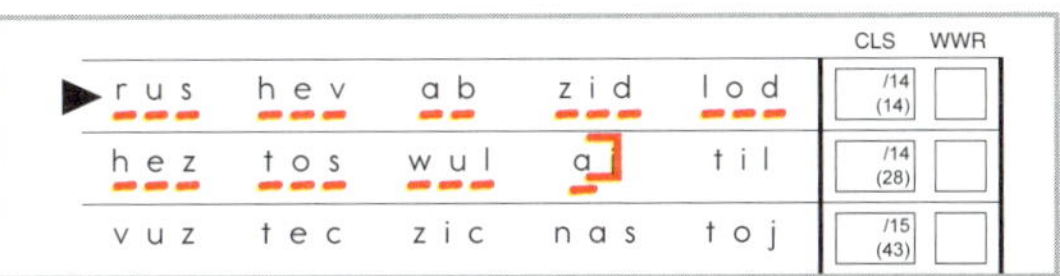

					CLS	WWR
r u s	h e v	a b	z i d	l o d	/14 (14)	
h e z	t o s	w u l	a j	t i l	/14 (28)	
v u z	t e c	z i c	n a s	t o j	/15 (43)	

Alyson: Fluency-Building Phase

Alyson is reading words the way we want all students to approach letter strings, even in kindergarten: by reading whole words accurately, without having to say the individual sounds first. She needs to increase automaticity to become more fluent at this approach.

					CLS	WWR
r u s	h e v	a b	z i d	l o d	/14 (14)	
h e z	t o s	w u l	a j	t i l	/14 (28)	
v u z	t e c	z i c	n a s	t o j	/15 (43)	

Nicholas: Generalization and Adaptation Phase

Nicholas can read VC and CVC letter strings as words effortlessly and automatically, without having to go sound by sound first. He can now apply this skill to reading text.

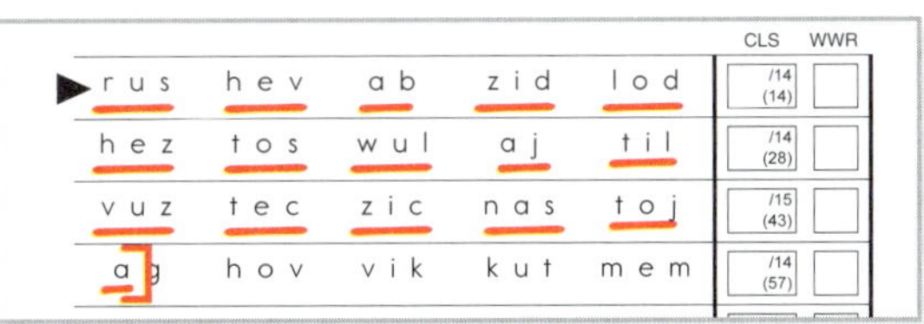

					CLS	WWR
r u s	h e v	a b	z i d	l o d	/14 (14)	
h e z	t o s	w u l	a j	t i l	/14 (28)	
v u z	t e c	z i c	n a s	t o j	/15 (43)	
a g	h o v	v i k	k u t	m e m	/14 (57)	

Next, take a look at the two Oral Reading Fluency scoring forms on the next page for Kyle and Logan, with the same Words Correct Per Minute scores. These forms show students at two points in the instructional hierarchy. The first form shows that Kyle is accurate but slow, and therefore needs instruction in reading fluency, while the second form shows that Logan is still in the acquisition phase and needs more instruction in accurate decoding. Fluency practice focused on rate would be a bad idea for this student!

Kyle

Accurate but slow—more fluency instruction needed

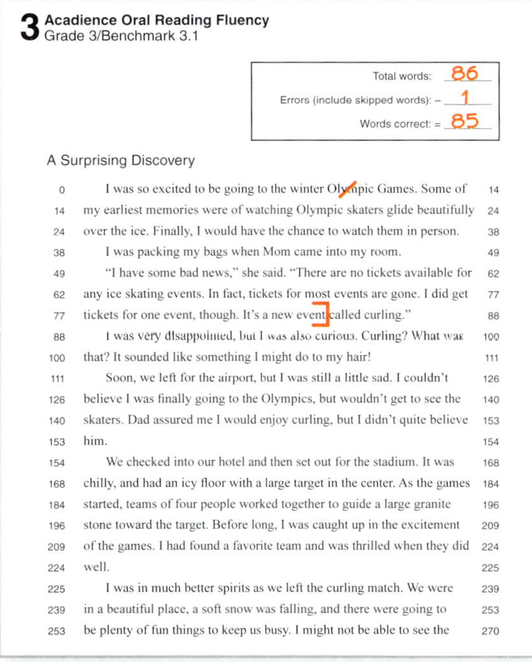

3 **Acadience Oral Reading Fluency**
Grade 3/Benchmark 3.1

Total words: 86
Errors (include skipped words): – 1
Words correct: = 85

A Surprising Discovery

0 I was so excited to be going to the winter Olympic Games. Some of 14
14 my earliest memories were of watching Olympic skaters glide beautifully 24
24 over the ice. Finally, I would have the chance to watch them in person. 38
38 I was packing my bags when Mom came into my room. 49
49 "I have some bad news," she said. "There are no tickets available for 62
62 any ice skating events. In fact, tickets for most events are gone. I did get 77
77 tickets for one event, though. It's a new event called curling." 88
88 I was very disappointed, but I was also curious. Curling? What was 100
100 that? It sounded like something I might do to my hair! 111
111 Soon, we left for the airport, but I was still a little sad. I couldn't 126
126 believe I was finally going to the Olympics, but wouldn't get to see the 140
140 skaters. Dad assured me I would enjoy curling, but I didn't quite believe 153
153 him. 154
154 We checked into our hotel and then set out for the stadium. It was 168
168 chilly, and had an icy floor with a large target in the center. As the games 184
184 started, teams of four people worked together to guide a large granite 196
196 stone toward the target. Before long, I was caught up in the excitement 209
209 of the games. I had found a favorite team and was thrilled when they did 224
224 well. 225
225 I was in much better spirits as we left the curling match. We were 239
239 in a beautiful place, a soft snow was falling, and there were going to 253
253 be plenty of fun things to keep us busy. I might not be able to see the 270

Logan

Inaccurate—more decoding instruction needed

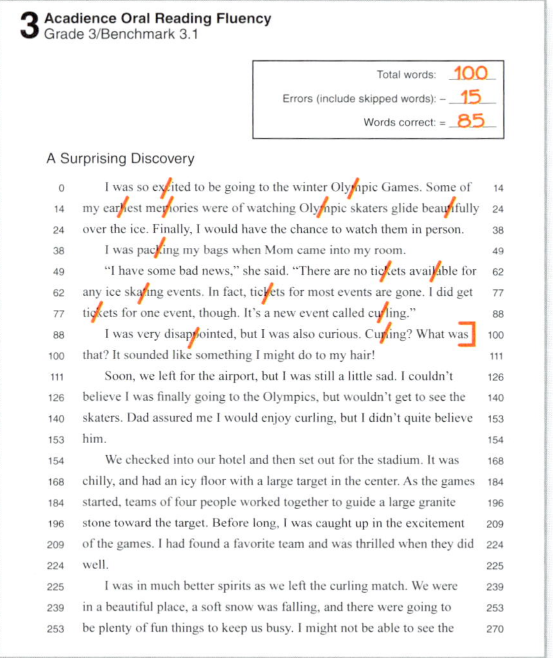

3 **Acadience Oral Reading Fluency**
Grade 3/Benchmark 3.1

Total words: 100
Errors (include skipped words): – 15
Words correct: = 85

A Surprising Discovery

0 I was so excited to be going to the winter Olympic Games. Some of 14
14 my earliest memories were of watching Olympic skaters glide beautifully 24
24 over the ice. Finally, I would have the chance to watch them in person. 38
38 I was packing my bags when Mom came into my room. 49
49 "I have some bad news," she said. "There are no tickets available for 62
62 any ice skating events. In fact, tickets for most events are gone. I did get 77
77 tickets for one event, though. It's a new event called curling." 88
88 I was very disappointed, but I was also curious. Curling? What was 100
100 that? It sounded like something I might do to my hair! 111
111 Soon, we left for the airport, but I was still a little sad. I couldn't 126
126 believe I was finally going to the Olympics, but wouldn't get to see the 140
140 skaters. Dad assured me I would enjoy curling, but I didn't quite believe 153
153 him. 154
154 We checked into our hotel and then set out for the stadium. It was 168
168 chilly, and had an icy floor with a large target in the center. As the games 184
184 started, teams of four people worked together to guide a large granite 196
196 stone toward the target. Before long, I was caught up in the excitement 209
209 of the games. I had found a favorite team and was thrilled when they did 224
224 well. 225
225 I was in much better spirits as we left the curling match. We were 239
239 in a beautiful place, a soft snow was falling, and there were going to 253
253 be plenty of fun things to keep us busy. I might not be able to see the 270

Oral Reading Fluency, Grade 3, Benchmark 3.1 from Acadience

Generate a Hypothesis

Generating a hypothesis may seem like an unnecessary step, but we've found that it is possible to create an intervention plan that is completely disconnected from the assessment data unless a clear hypothesis statement concludes the findings of the assessment.

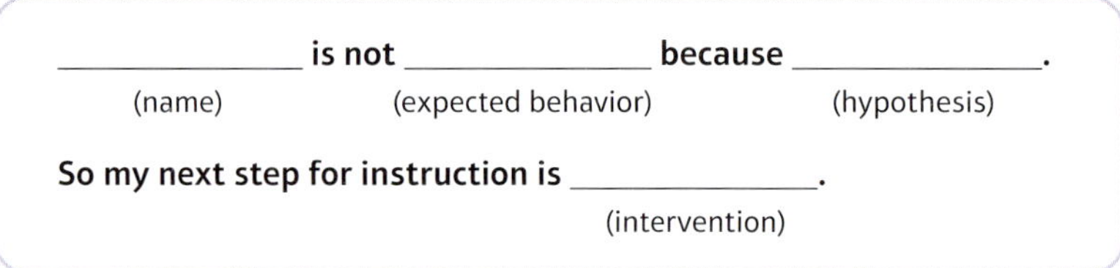

_______________ is not _______________ because _______________.
(name) (expected behavior) (hypothesis)

So my next step for instruction is _______________.
(intervention)

The chart below shows a variety of hypothesis statements. Each hypothesis is informed by collecting diagnostic assessment data during Step 2 of the Collaborative Improvement Cycle (CIC): Gap Analysis.

	Hypothesis	Next Step for Instruction
1	**John is not comprehending grade-level text because he can't accurately read the words.**	Teach decoding
2	**Sophia is not comprehending grade-level text because she can't fluently read the words.**	Build fluency in text
3	**Carlos is not comprehending grade-level text because he doesn't know the meanings of the words.**	Teach vocabulary
4	**Tu is not comprehending grade-level text because he is accurate with letter sounds but not fluent with reading basic CVC words.**	Teach automatic blending
5	**Reyna is not able to read basic CVC words because she doesn't know letter-sound relationships.**	Teach letter sounds and blending
6	**DJ is not able to read basic CVC words because he can't segment phonemes.**	Teach phoneme segmentation, letter sounds, and blending

It seems obvious, right? But believe us, it can be easy to jump straight from "the student can't comprehend" to implementing an intervention. You will waste precious time if you don't target the intervention to fill the exact skill gap for each student. Spending time collecting and analyzing diagnostic data is time well spent because it helps you quickly determine the right intervention for each student.

In Closing, Remember...

Completing diagnostic assessments gives you an idea of where to begin instruction with each student's specific skill gaps. But the discussion doesn't stop there.

In Chapter 6, we talk about progress-monitoring assessment: how to effectively monitor progress when you're intervening with students, so you can be prepared for that step.

In Chapter 7, we describe the final type of assessment: Outcome Assessment.

In Chapter 8, we help you dive further into data by providing guidelines on implementing effective instruction based on student needs.

CHAPTER 6

Progress Monitoring

Is the Instruction Working?

Progress monitoring involves the repeated measurement of a skill that is the focus of instruction to help determine whether to continue the instruction or change it. Think of progress monitoring as a feedback loop to you, the teacher, about your instruction. It allows you to track learning on a graph over time so you know whether you should continue what and how you are teaching or make a change.

What Are Characteristics of a Quality Progress-Monitoring Assessment?

- **It can be administered quickly—often in just one minute.**
- **It is given under standardized testing conditions—the same conditions every time we give one.**
- **It provides reliable and valid indicators within essential skill areas.**

Sound familiar so far? Many characteristics of a good progress-monitoring tool are identical to those of a quality universal screening assessment (see Chapter 4). But here's the difference: Screening assessments need to predict future reading performance, whereas progress-monitoring tools must do that, too, but also have the next two characteristics:

PROGRESS MONITORING

ANALOGY: GPS
(Where are you? Where do you want to go? And are you on track?)

Step	Key Question	Assessment Purpose
1. Gap Identification	• Which students and systems need help? • What is the gap between actual and desired outcomes?	Universal Screening
2. Gap Analysis	• What should be taught and how? • Why is the gap happening?	Diagnostic Assessment
3. Action Planning	• What is the plan to close the gap?	
4. Outcome Analysis	• Is the instruction working?	Progress Monitoring
	• Did the instruction work?	Outcome Assessment

- **They are sensitive to change over short periods of time.** Progress-monitoring data are displayed on a graph showing student performance on a single skill over time, under different teaching conditions. By assessing and tracking that skill over time, it is possible to see whether students are making gains.
- **They include multiple forms for assessing the same task, at the same level of difficulty.** A progress-monitoring assessment is not made up of just pre- and post-tests or a couple of check-ins. The tools we recommend include up to 20 different forms at the same level of difficulty, which can be used over time. Why? Because decisions about student learning based on multiple data points across time are more accurate than decisions based on performance at a single point in time (Good et al., 2019). Furthermore, we know student outcomes improve when teachers use graphed progress-monitoring data to inform their instruction (Stecker et al., 2005).

Examples of Progress-Monitoring Assessments

- Acadience
- DIBELS 8th Edition
- FastBridge
- aimswebPlus
- easyCBM

Learn more about progress-monitoring mistakes to avoid from Stephanie here.

How Progress Monitoring Fits Into MTSS

Progress monitoring is one of four types of assessments that are required for implementing Multi-Tiered System of Support (MTSS). We use progress-monitoring data to decide whether to move students from one tier to another. For example, we might move students who are not making the same progress as others during small-group instruction to a more intensive tier of support. On the other hand, we might fade or reduce support for students who have met their goals. And we might suggest special education services for students who only make progress with intensive and individualized intervention. We also use progress-monitoring data to decide if our tiers of instructional support are effective. For example, we might make improvements to Tier 2 intervention if no one who receives it is catching up to the goals.

Two Types of Progress Monitoring

The progress monitoring we're talking about is not just about making sure students are on track. It is a more formal assessment that's different from informal tools teachers often use to monitor student learning, though both formal and informal assessments play a role in instructional decision-making.

Curriculum-Based Measurement (CBM)

A CBM measures student performance on indicators of overall reading health, captures growth over time, and predicts future reading health. Progress monitoring with CBM allows us to track progress over time.

Mastery Monitoring Assessment

Most teachers give assessments—or regular check-ins—to see if students have learned what they've taught. These tests may be part of published instructional or intervention programs. They are called mastery monitoring assessments because they allow us to assess for mastery of specific content that was taught. For example, we might have students read and write a list of words from a recent phonics lesson and determine the percent of correct answers each student gets.

Mastery monitoring measures a student's understanding and proficiency in a target skill, and we use the results to determine whether to move to the next skill in a sequence, reteach it, or intensify support during instruction.

The University of Florida Literacy Institute (UFLI) uses the term "progress monitoring" for the weekly check-ins in its Foundations program, and that's certainly accurate: By checking in on the skills you taught in a given week (in the case of UFLI, with a sound, word, and sentence dictation), you are indeed seeing how each child is responding to the curriculum. The weekly UFLI assessments are examples of mastery monitoring measures. They answer the question, "Did the student learn what I just taught?" They don't answer the question, "Is the student on track to be an okay reader in the future?" That is what a CBM is for. Tools created by schools, districts, or states are likely to be mastery monitoring assessments.

Both types of assessments are useful. Mastery monitoring informs decisions about progress through a series of lessons (Did students learn what I just taught?), and CBM informs decisions about overall growth across lessons (Are students learning what I am teaching?).

Throughout the rest of the book, when we refer to "progress monitoring," we mean CBM.

Similarities and Differences

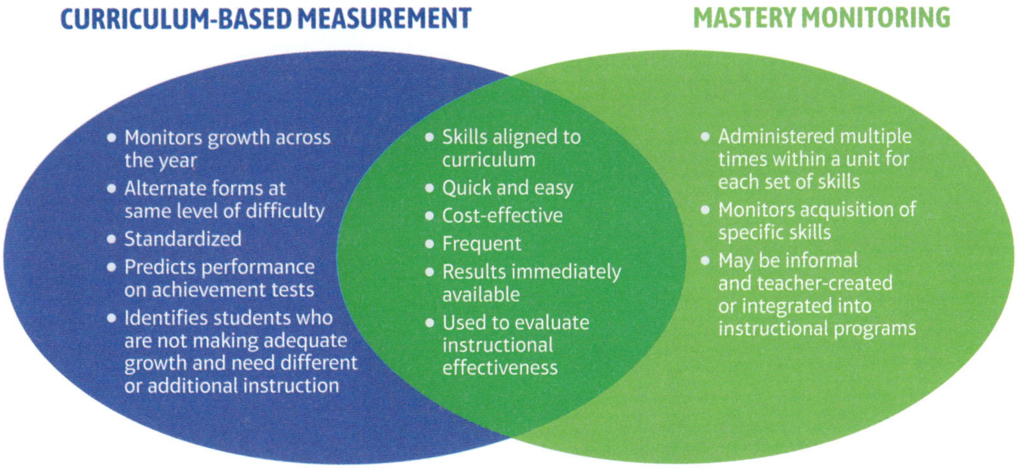

CURRICULUM-BASED MEASUREMENT

- Monitors growth across the year
- Alternate forms at same level of difficulty
- Standardized
- Predicts performance on achievement tests
- Identifies students who are not making adequate growth and need different or additional instruction

Both

- Skills aligned to curriculum
- Quick and easy
- Cost-effective
- Frequent
- Results immediately available
- Used to evaluate instructional effectiveness

MASTERY MONITORING

- Administered multiple times within a unit for each set of skills
- Monitors acquisition of specific skills
- May be informal and teacher-created or integrated into instructional programs

How to Create a Progress-Monitoring Graph

When you can clearly visualize your progress-monitoring data, as compared to your goal, it's much easier to celebrate success and make instructional decisions. Here are the steps to setting up your graph:

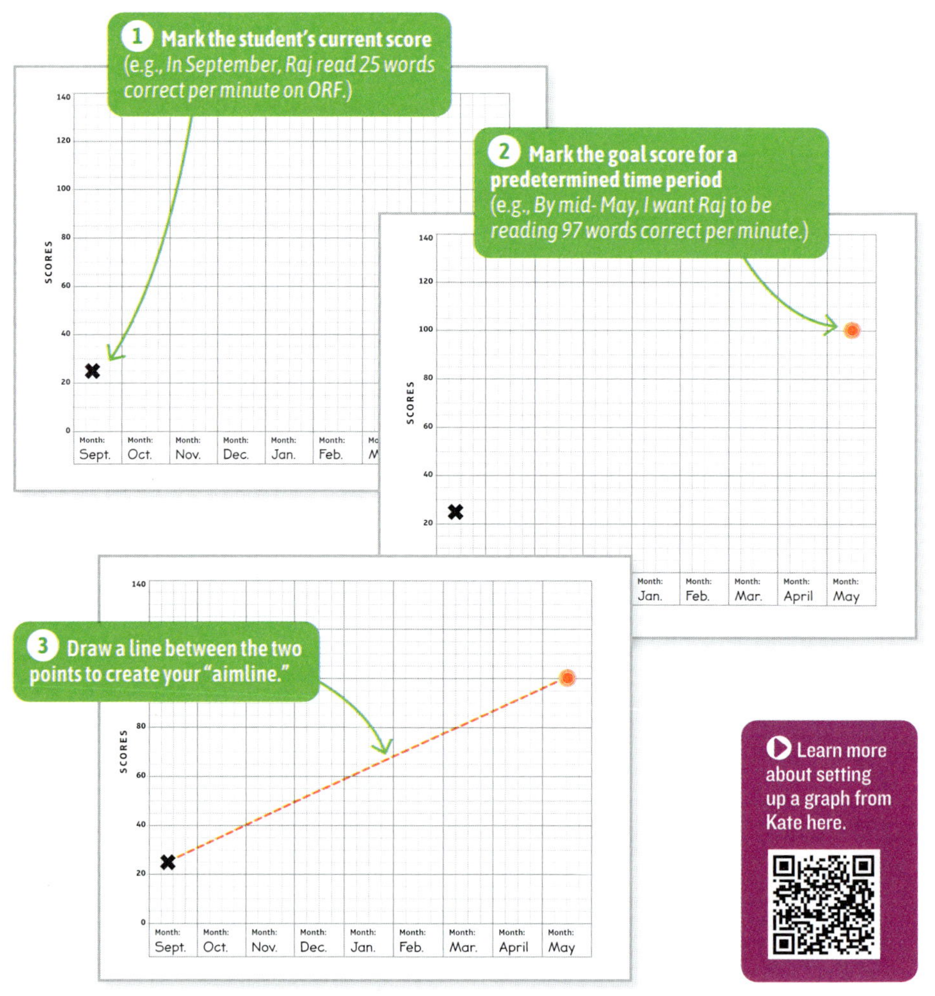

Learn more about setting up a graph from Kate here.

In Chapter 8, we present several examples of progress-monitoring graphs with data and talk about how we would use that data to inform our instruction.

Kate

"At the risk of sounding like a complete data nerd (even more than I already do!), I proudly admit that I get a high from watching my students' progress-monitoring data climb. Seeing student scores increase after instruction targets their needs is extremely empowering and brings me joy. This chapter gives you everything you need to know about progress monitoring so you can experience that empowerment and joy for yourself."

Who Should Administer Progress-Monitoring Assessments?

Generally, the person most directly responsible for teaching the student should monitor progress, but anyone who has been trained in this type of assessment can do it, too, which might include paraprofessionals, special education staff, reading specialists, school psychologists, and speech pathologists. You won't be surprised to learn that Kate insists on doing it herself! Regardless of who collects the data, whoever is working with a student should have access to that data and the progress-monitoring graph created from it.

Learn more about administering progress-monitoring assessments from Stephanie here.

Points to Keep in Mind When Progress Monitoring

1 Monitor the skill you are teaching

Some students may score below benchmark on universal screenings in several areas. The lowest skill for which a student has not yet met the goal should be the first target of instruction, and the progress-monitoring assessment should match that skill. For example, a third-grade student may score low during universal screening on reading comprehension, text reading rate, and text-reading accuracy. The lowest skill in the skill sequence is accurate reading or decoding, so that is the target of instruction, and the progress-monitoring assessment would be Oral Reading Fluency (ORF) Accuracy.

Although universal screening at benchmark periods should always be done with materials that match the grade level a student is assigned to, progress monitoring can be done with below-level or above-level materials, depending on what instruction the child is receiving. Older students who are missing foundational skills will need instruction in below-grade-level skills, and, therefore, progress-monitoring materials should be below grade level.

For example, if you're working on comprehension with a third-grade student who is struggling with reading, you need to assess backwards, or survey back, to find the lowest skill the student hasn't yet mastered. Is it:

- Automaticity with third-grade texts?
- Accuracy with third-grade texts?
- Accuracy with second- or even first-grade texts?
- Basic decoding?
- Phonemic awareness?

In Chapter 8, we share a flowchart to help you determine a target skill.

You can't progress monitor this third-grade student with the third-grade ORF passage if you're working on accuracy in texts at a first-grade level, or working on segmenting phonemes. When we monitor students using material that is too difficult for them, we will not see growth in short intervals of time. This could lead us to believe that our instruction isn't working when that actually isn't the case. Because the gap between what we're teaching and what we're measuring is so large, we can't pick up on changes in the target skill.

2 Monitor using only one progress-monitoring measure at a time

When a student scores below expectation on screening in more than one area, choose the progress-monitoring measure that matches that lowest skill being targeted for instruction.

Example 1: In a midyear screening, kindergarten student Nidia scored below benchmark in Phoneme Segmentation Fluency (PSF) and Nonsense Word Fluency (NWF). Her teacher would make phonemic awareness and phonics the first instructional targets, using PSF for progress monitoring. Once she meets that goal, the progress monitoring can shift to NWF.

Example 2: In the middle of first grade, Declan scores low on both NWF and ORF. His teacher would focus instruction on the alphabetic principle and basic phonics (which is indicated by NWF), using NWF for progress monitoring. Once Declan meets both NWF goals, instruction should focus on reading connected text with accuracy and automaticity, using ORF for progress monitoring.

Example 3: In the middle of third grade, Asher scores low on ORF Retell, Words Correct, and Accuracy, so his teacher conducts a Survey Level Assessment as described in Chapter 5. She finds he has difficulty reading second-grade and even first-grade ORF materials accurately, fluently, and for meaning, so she gives him NWF and PSF assessments, on which he scores below benchmark. As such,

Asher's teacher focuses instruction on phonemic awareness and phonics and uses PSF for progress monitoring.

3 Set ambitious goals to close the gap

When we have students who are far behind in reading, we can't just hope they'll make one year of progress every year, or they'll always remain behind! We don't want to set unreasonably high goals, which will lead to frustration and failure.

In general, progress-monitoring goals should be ambitious enough to close the gap and catch students up to the grade-level expectations. They should also be individual to each student. Tools such as Pathways of Progress from Acadience Learning and Zones of Growth from DIBELS 8th Edition can guide goal setting based on normative growth goals or the level of progress made in the past by students who scored the same as your student at the beginning of the year.

Goal-setting considerations for the beginning of the year:

- If you are using grade-level material for progress monitoring, use the goal for the next benchmark period (e.g., middle of year) as your progress-monitoring goal. If focusing on ORF scores, the accuracy benchmark should be your first goal, and then the automaticity (words correct per minute) benchmark goal.
- If you are using below-grade-level material for instruction and progress monitoring, use the end-of-year goal for the measure you are monitoring, but cut the timeline in half, as described in Chapter 5.
- If you're monitoring students using below-grade materials, set short-term and long-term goals for them. When they reach the first short-term goal, move them to the next level of progress-monitoring material and set a new goal.

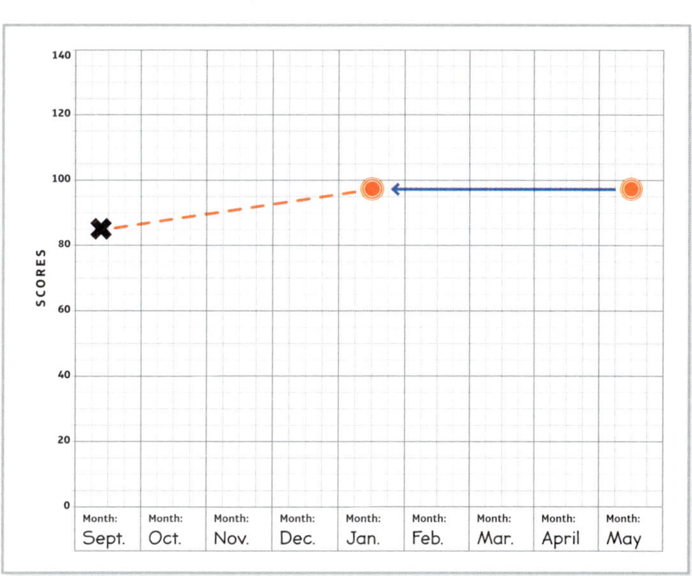

Example: Third-grade student Briane scored well below benchmark for Oral Reading Fluency at the beginning of the year.

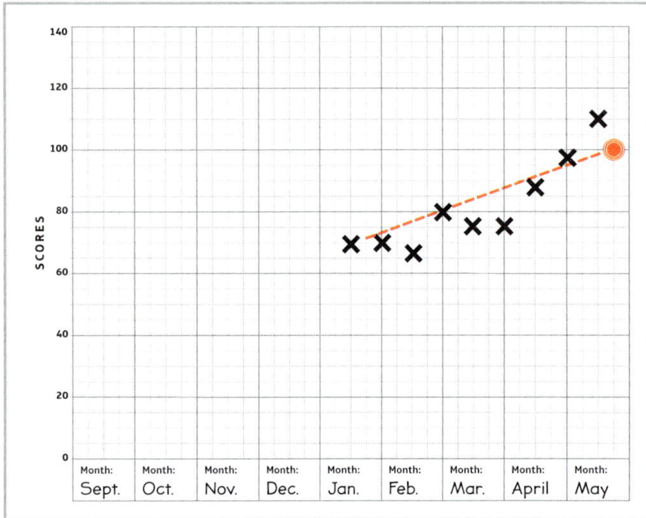

Briane's first goal (as seen in the graph on the previous page): By the middle of the year, she will read second-grade text orally at a rate of 87 or more words correct per minute, with at least 97 percent accuracy, and be able to talk about what she has read, using at least 27 words in the retell.

Briane's second goal (as seen in the graph on the left): By the end of the year, she will read third-grade text orally at a rate of 100 or more words correct per minute, with at least 97 percent accuracy, and be able to talk about what she has read with at least 30 words in the retell. She will read grade-level text silently for meaning with a Maze adjusted score of at least 19.

How Often Should I Monitor Progress?

There are no firm rules about how often to monitor progress, but we use the intensity of the instructional support to help us determine frequency. Students who are getting reading intervention don't have a day to waste on instruction that isn't helping, so frequent progress monitoring is warranted.

At the heart of progress monitoring is the feedback it provides to inform instruction—so if you aren't willing to change your instruction, there's no point wasting time on monitoring progress!

The first time Kate saw Stephanie present was in 2022. The title of Stephanie's talk was, "Weighing the Hog Doesn't Make It Fatter" (an expression she heard years ago related to progress monitoring), indicating that just because you measure something often doesn't mean it leads to the desired growth. When it comes to reading assessment, the expression is a reminder that testing students repeatedly isn't going to improve their skills. First we screen, then we use the screening data to target instruction, and then we monitor progress—and continue to use data to target instruction as needed.

Many states and districts require teachers to go directly from screening to progress monitoring but *don't* require instruction in between...and then educational leaders are surprised when scores don't climb!

Furthermore, some states and districts require all students who score below benchmark on universal screeners to be monitored twice a month, which we don't believe is necessary.

You need at least five to seven data points to see a trend on a progress-monitoring graph (more on this in Chapter 8). For students working on below-grade-level skills, and receiving intensive intervention, time is of the essence, and weekly progress monitoring is needed to see the trend (Are more of the data points above or below the aimline? What direction are they generally going?) in five to seven weeks.

For students working on grade-level skills, it might be enough to monitor their progress every other week for 10 weeks and then decide about changes to instruction.

For her kindergartners, Kate finds that every other week is frequent enough to get the data she needs to monitor students who are not far from the goal, working on grade-level skills, and receiving her support within the regular classroom, as opposed to intensive intervention.

You definitely need to monitor more frequently when students' skills are far below grade level—as frequently as necessary to determine if you should continue the current instruction or make a change. Weekly progress monitoring usually makes sense in this situation. Within five weeks, you will have a trend that shows you if what you're doing is working. As shown in the graphs below, the more often you collect progress-monitoring data, the faster you can make a decision about whether or not you need to change instruction.

If monitoring once a week is good, is monitoring more often even better? Actually, no—monitoring more than once a week takes time away from instruction, without providing any additional information on a child's progress.

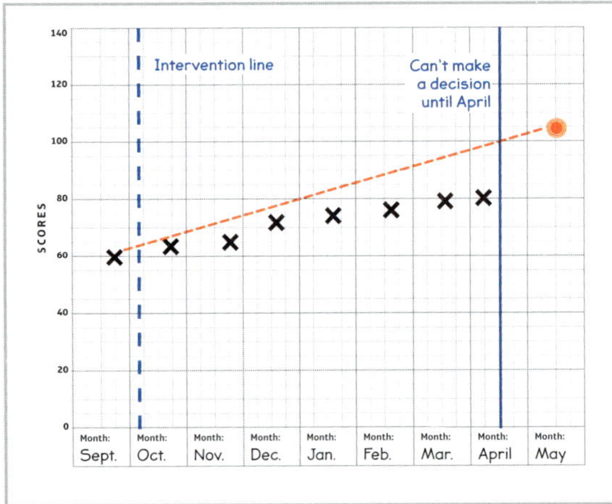

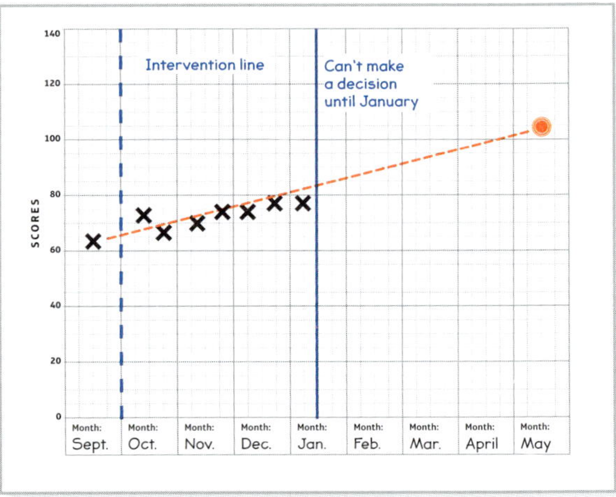

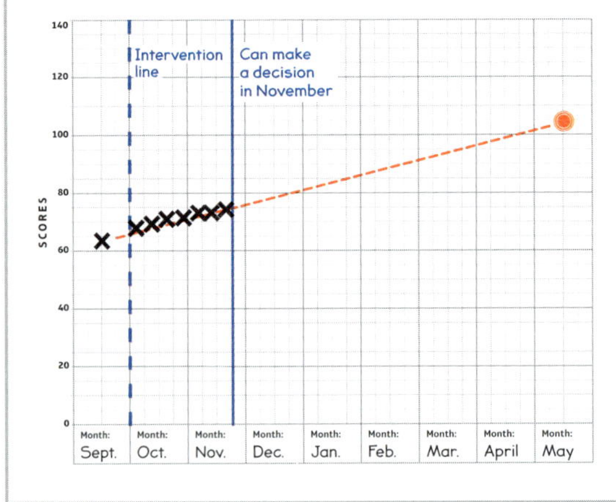

(top left) If monitoring monthly, it will take almost the whole school year to have enough data points to see a trend.

(top right) If monitoring twice a month, it will take a whole semester to see a trend.

(bottom left) Weekly progress monitoring facilitates immediate decision-making.

If students are below benchmark on only the Maze assessment, and that's what you're using to monitor progress (because they were at benchmark in all of the preceding skills), we recommend using it no more than every other week, as it's less sensitive to growth than other measures.

How Can I Find Time to Monitor All of These Students?

If you're asking yourself that question, a better question may be: *Should* I be monitoring them all?

If more than 20 percent of your class scores below benchmark on the screening assessment, you may want to consider ways to improve the match between students' skills and classroom reading instruction before intervening and beginning progress monitoring with individual students.

If you find half of your class is at risk, progress monitoring that many students would be overwhelming. You may want to select a few students you're most worried about to monitor (e.g., those who were well below benchmark), but also spend some time analyzing and improving Tier 1 curriculum and instruction. Administrative mandates requiring progress-monitoring frequency based on universal screening results rob teachers of Tier 1 planning and instruction time by emphasizing measurement rather than instruction.

If you have a daily intervention group (let's say it's made up of five students) and want to monitor them weekly, we suggest that you don't take group time every Friday to do progress monitoring. Continue to take the students for small-group instruction every day, and assess one of them at the end of the period every Monday, another student every Tuesday, etc. This cuts every session down by just a couple of minutes and still provides five days of small-group time each week.

In Closing, Remember...

Progress monitoring is about finding out if instruction is working or needs to change.

It is a powerful instructional tool. But simply putting dots on a graph isn't the important part. We can monitor students every day and their reading skills won't necessarily improve. Those skills will improve only when studying that graph leads to informed decisions about instruction. Be sure to schedule time to review the graph of any student you are monitoring and take the necessary action, which we talk about in Chapter 8!

CHAPTER 7

Outcome Assessment

Did the Instruction Work?

At the point you expect students to have mastered a set of content, outcome assessments tell you whether they have achieved that goal. It is used at Step 4 of the Collaborative Improvement Cycle (CIC): Outcome Analysis.

Outcome assessments are typically given at the end of a unit or course. In the United States and Canada, reading achievement tests are often *high-stakes* outcome assessments, meaning they are used to hold students and schools accountable for teaching and learning. Two types of data we prefer to use for outcome assessments are data from student assessments and adult implementation data.

Data From Student Outcome Assessments

Student outcome assessments are somewhat helpful for summarizing the learning of individual students and even more useful for evaluating the effectiveness of instructional systems. In the next section, we explain three sources of student outcome data:

- reading achievement tests
- screening data (using the percent at benchmark on screening results)
- progress-monitoring data (using the percent meeting goals on progress-monitoring assessments)

OUTCOME ASSESSMENT

ANALOGY: Rearview mirror (These summative assessments tell us where we have been with our students.)

Step	Key Question	Assessment Purpose
1. Gap Identification	• Which students and systems need help? • What is the gap between actual and desired outcomes?	Universal Screening
2. Gap Analysis	• What should be taught and how? • Why is the gap happening?	Diagnostic Assessment
3. Action Planning	• What is the plan to close the gap?	
4. Outcome Analysis	• Is the instruction working?	Progress Monitoring
	• Did the instruction work?	Outcome Assessment

Reading Achievement Tests

The most common outcome assessments are reading achievement tests. There are two main types of reading achievement tests: formal, norm-referenced and informal, classroom-based.

Formal, Norm-Referenced Reading Achievement Tests

Examples of formal, norm-referenced reading achievement tests used for outcome assessment include the Terra Nova, the SAT-10, and the state and provincial assessments used in the United States and Canada, usually in grades 3–8. These assessments measure whether students met the reading and English language arts standards for each grade.

Formal reading achievement tests are typically given in the spring, toward the end of the school year. Scores are usually reported as stanines or percentiles relative to state, provincial, or national norms. In the United States, results are typically described as advanced, proficient, basic, and below basic. Although the same terms may be used across states, the expectations or cut scores for each grade vary by state. For example, one state may expect students to read words with vowel teams by the end of second grade, while another state may not expect it until the middle of third grade. In other words, the difficulty level of achievement tests is not the same from state to state.

In an effort to hold schools accountable for reading achievement, many states use test results to determine schools that receive school-improvement support and funding. That may seem like a reasonable practice on the surface, but such accountability systems have had negative outcomes, such as pausing instruction for test prep, retaining students in their current grade, and putting pressure on teachers who teach grades in which state tests are given.

While it may be useful to know the percentage of students who didn't do well on the achievement test, a percentage doesn't give you the kind of information you need to plan effective intervention for low-scoring students. Unfortunately, the results often are not available to teachers until late summer or even the fall of the next school year. Planning instruction is best accomplished with the screening and diagnostic assessments, which we discussed in earlier chapters.

Perhaps the best use of formal, norm-referenced assessments is for planning grade-level and school-level instruction at the start of the school year, as a team. If the outcomes weren't good last year, you can teach the standards differently in hopes of getting better results. For example, if only a small percent of your fourth graders could summarize a passage on the state test, the fourth-grade teachers may teach summarization differently and/or more carefully the next year.

In Ontario, where Kate teaches, elementary schools use the Education Quality and Accountability Office (EQAO) assessment to test reading (along with writing and math) at the end of third grade and sixth grade. Kate spent several years teaching third grade, and each fall she and her colleagues would gather to discuss and analyze the EQAO results from the previous spring. While student-level data (though rarely a surprise) was most helpful to the fourth-grade teachers who were now teaching these students, Kate found that looking at broad patterns helped her to plan her third-grade instruction. For example, when more than half of the students answered a question about literary devices incorrectly, she knew she needed to be more intentional with that topic moving forward.

Informal, Classroom-Based Reading Achievement Tests

Examples of informal, classroom-based reading achievement tests include unit tests provided by curriculum publishers and teacher-created tests.

You are probably giving these tests all the time but not thinking of them as outcome assessments. At the end of a unit or series of lessons, most teachers give tests provided in their reading program or ones they create themselves to judge whether students have learned what they were taught. These tests are likely connected to grade-level standards or curriculum expectations, and provide data to determine report-card grades.

We want you to think deeply about these assessments. As we have recommended throughout the book, don't collect data you aren't going to use. What happens when you give a test and find that most students in your class didn't pass? Do you move on anyway? Or do you use the information to inform your teaching going forward? If you aren't going to respond to the data, don't give the assessment in the first place.

Screening Data as Outcome Assessment

In Chapter 4, we explored universal screening assessment as a way to identify students who are struggling or may struggle in the future so instruction, even intensive intervention, can be provided early. Universal screening can also be used as an outcome assessment to answer the question, "Did we meet our goal of increasing the percentage of students who are on track for reading?" It can help you determine if each student in your class met the end-of-year benchmark goal or at least closed the gap by moving from well-below to below benchmark.

You can also compare the percentage of students who scored at the end-of-year benchmark goal to the goal percent you set after the beginning- or middle-of-year screening. For example, if 45 percent of a first-grade teacher's class meets benchmark on the Acadience Reading Composite Score at the beginning of the year, she might set a goal of 70 percent for the middle of the year and 90 percent for the end of the year.

You might want to work in grade-level teams to use the percentage of students in the grade who scored at benchmark on universal screening at the middle and end of the year as an outcome assessment. All teachers in the grade would be looking for an increase in the percentage of students in the grade who scored at the benchmark goals. For example, it is not uncommon for the percentage of students at benchmark to go from roughly 40 percent at the beginning of the year to 60 percent at the middle of the year and 80 percent at the end of the year. See the overview report on the next page for an example of using screening data to review outcomes.

Grade 1 Overview Report

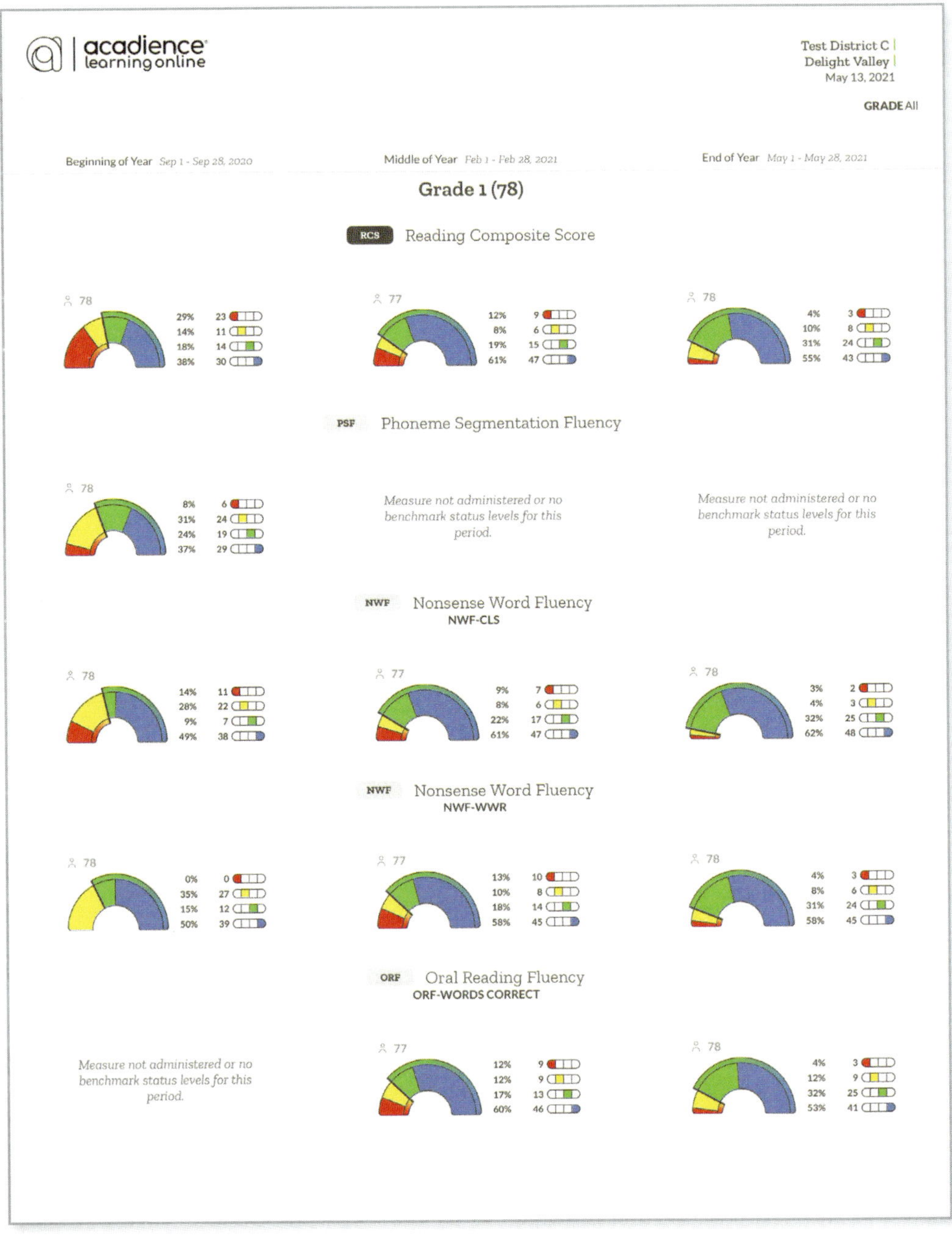

Acadience

Burning Question

Should we use screening data as grades on a report card?

Report cards can be an excellent tool for communicating with parents and guardians. They enable us to share student progress and expectations at regular intervals across the school year. Results from all forms of assessment—universal screening, diagnostic assessment, progress monitoring, and outcome assessment—can be used to inform the grades you assign students. The authors of assessments such as Acadience Reading advise against using the universal screening scores in high-stakes ways, such as report card grades (e.g., "below benchmark" automatically means a "C" grade in reading). Again, just use them as one piece of the puzzle to inform the grades you give. For example, on a report card entry about reading grade-level text for meaning, rather than entering the ORF WCPM score or score status (at/above, below or well below benchmark), consider that information along with performance on other classroom reading tasks. You can also use data from assessments to inform your comments about students' strengths (e.g., "Ben can accurately and automatically read words with the consonant vowel consonant [CVC] pattern"), as well as your next steps (e.g., "A goal for Naomi is for her to read grade-level text automatically enough so that she can focus on understanding what she reads.")

Progress-Monitoring Data as Outcome Assessment

Like screening data, you can use progress-monitoring data to measure outcomes. Small-group intervention takes a lot of resources (especially human), and we need to know if that investment is paying off. One way to do that is to pull the progress-monitoring data together for students who are getting the same small-group intervention. What we're looking for is the percentage of students in each small group who reached, or are on track to reach, the goal from their intervention plan.

The chart below shows progress-monitoring data for four students who received the same small-group intervention. Three of the students (75 percent) made accelerated progress and caught up to the goal, but one did not. Data like these illustrate the effectiveness of the intervention and show how aggregate small-group progress-monitoring data can be used as outcome assessment.

Group 1 Progress Check

Student	Rate of Progress	Met Goal?
Carly	above typical	Yes
Claire	above typical	Yes
Curtis	above typical	Yes
Conrad	below typical	No

We encourage you to work with grade-level colleagues to review the percentage of students in the grade who received small-group intervention and reached their goals. For example, if you set a goal for 80 percent of the students receiving small-group intervention to reach benchmark, and less than 80 percent of them do, it may be time to cycle back to Steps 1 to 3 of the Collaborative Improvement Cycle (CIC) and revise your plan, develop a different hypothesis, or more carefully identify the gap or define the problem.

Looking at student outcome data only tells part of the story. For the full story, and to determine where to go next, you need to know if the adults implemented what they planned. This is called adult implementation data.

Adult Implementation Data

Thinking about and tracking whether adults in charge of instruction did what they planned may be a new concept for you. It may even feel beyond your reach. That's okay! We want to plant the seeds that will help you become more targeted and efficient when it comes to reading instruction and intervention.

If you went to the trouble of thinking carefully about what your students need and developing a plan to improve their reading performance, wouldn't you want to be sure the plan was implemented with fidelity? After all, it's impossible to say whether the plan worked unless you're confident it was executed as designed.

Implementation fidelity is the degree to which an intervention or treatment is carried out as planned, intended, or originally designed (Gresham, 1989, 2004; Gresham et al., 2000), and it can be applied to all three tiers of instruction in a school. Hagermoser and colleagues (2009) call it treatment integrity and define it as "the extent to which essential intervention components are delivered in a comprehensive and consistent manner by an interventionist trained to deliver the intervention."

In experimental research, it is important to demonstrate that changes in student learning are the result of implementing an intervention. When we have evidence that the intervention was implemented as planned, we can be confident that the intervention was responsible for student learning (or lack thereof), and not some other factor.

Implementation fidelity is a well-established requirement in the research community. But what are its implications for classroom reading instruction?

Stephanie "Early in my career, I was called in to consult on a third-grade student who was not making progress in basic decoding. The student's progress-monitoring graph was as flat as a parking lot. I had been in the problem-solving meetings about this student, so I knew the team had carefully analyzed the gap and created an intervention plan that was targeted to meet the student's needs. After six weeks without any growth, we reconvened and spent several hours refining the intervention only to discover that the plan had never been implemented in the first place. The interventionist spent the first 10 days gathering instructional materials, the classroom teacher often forgot to send the student for intervention, and both the student and interventionist had been absent several days. No wonder there wasn't any growth! If we had asked a few basic questions when we saw no growth on the graph, we could have saved everyone a lot of time!"

Learn more about implementation fidelity from Stephanie here.

Instructional Implementation Checklist

Teacher: ______________________ Date: ____________ Time: ____________

Program: ______________________ Observer: ______________________

Teacher Behavior	YES	NO	NA
1. Clear instruction at brisk pace: ☐ YES ☐ SOMETIMES ☐ NO			
a. Provides clear directions			
b. Teaches the program			
c. Moves quickly between tasks with adequate think time			
2. Elicits responses: ☐ YES ☐ SOMETIMES ☐ NO			
a. Uses active response procedures (choral, partner, written)			
b. Provides think time			
3. Monitors student performance: ☐ YES ☐ SOMETIMES ☐ NO			
a. Circulates around the room			
b. Listens carefully to oral responses			
c. Looks carefully at written responses			
4. Provides feedback and adjusts lesson: ☐ YES ☐ SOMETIMES ☐ NO			
a. Timely error correction			
b. Additional practice follows error correction			
c. Positive feedback for correct responses and/or effort			
d. Redirects misbehavior			
e. Connects with students by making eye contact, using their names, greeting them, smiling			

Student Behavior	YES	NO	NA
1. Active participation with accurate responses: ☐ YES ☐ SOMETIMES ☐ NO When requested, the student does the following:			
a. Respond to prompts			
b. Respond accurately			
c. Work with partners			
d. Read orally			
e. Read text accurately			
f. Read silently			
g. Write answers			
2. Attention during instruction: ☐ YES ☐ SOMETIMES ☐ NO			
a. Look at the teacher			
b. Look at the stimulus			

Directions for use:

- Mark a tally in the Yes box as each teacher or student behavior is
- Mark a tally in the No box when an opportunity for a teacher or student behavior is presented but not observed
- Circle yes or no in the top row headings for each behavior based on where the majority of tally marks are placed at the end of the observation
- For each of the 4 teacher behaviors and 2 student behaviors circle yes sometimes or no
- Identify any follow-up coaching needed:
  - Maintenance check in
  - Minimal feedback and follow up
  - Moderate feedback, planning and follow up
  - Planning, modeling, we do, and follow up

Based on the work of MiMTSS TA Center and Oregon RTI

Combining Student Outcome Assessment and Adult Implementation Data

The chart below, based on the work of Harlacher, Collins, and Potter (2024), represents four possible results of outcome assessment, depending on whether the plan was implemented with fidelity and if it was successful. As you review the chart, remember, outcome data tells you if students met the goal you and your colleagues set for them and adult implementation data tells you if you and your colleagues implemented your plan with fidelity.

The case examples below illustrate the four possible results of outcome assessment and implementation data. For each example, you'll find a student example and a systems example.

		Student Outcome Data	
		Met the Goal	**Didn't Meet the Goal**
Adult Implementation Data	**Implemented the Plan**	**Jackpot!** Cases 1 and 2	**Back to the drawing board!** Cases 3 and 4
	Didn't Implement the Plan	**You got lucky!** Cases 5 and 6	**Time to break down barriers!** Cases 7 and 8

JACKPOT! Implemented the Plan, Met the Goal

This is the best-case scenario—the outcome we hope for every time we engage in the CIC. You know you're getting somewhere when you implement the plan and it works to improve reading outcomes!

Case 1: Student Example

Outcome Goal: By the middle of the year, Johnny will read 35 words correctly per minute on second-grade ORF passages, as a result of receiving a repeated-reading intervention three times a week.

Mrs. Hunter is a reading interventionist who supports second-graders. She noticed that Johnny scored low on Oral Reading Fluency (ORF) Words Correct (WC) on the beginning-of-year screening. She attended a professional development workshop where she learned about the effectiveness of repeated-reading intervention for students who struggle to read fluently, and she wanted to try it with Johnny. She reviewed his data and noticed that he met the ORF Accuracy goal but not the WC goal, making him a perfect candidate for a repeated-reading intervention. She set a goal for him to increase his ORF WC score by 25 points by the middle-of-year screening. She was thrilled when weekly progress monitoring revealed his ORF WC score increasing. Her next step: fade the frequency of the intervention.

Case 2: Systems Example

Outcome Goal: By the middle of the year, 65 percent of the first graders will read nonwords correctly on a Nonsense Word Fluency (NWF) assessment, without sounding them out.

At the beginning-of-year screening, only 35 percent of the first-grade students at Acme Elementary scored at or above benchmark on NWF. The first-grade teachers decided to seek support from the special education, EL, and gifted staff for assistance in teaching Tier 1 phonics and spelling in skill-based, teacher-led groups. They were thrilled to see that 68 percent of the students met the NWF goals on the middle-of-year screening. When the team revisited their action plan, they saw that they had implemented what they planned, including differentiating their ELA block, using an explicit and systematic program, and having every student taught by an adult. The first-grade teachers celebrated their win and rolled up their sleeves to continue helping all students reach the benchmark goals by the end of the year.

BACK TO THE DRAWING BOARD!

Implemented the Plan, Didn't Meet the Goal

It can be frustrating to implement your plan and miss your goals—very frustrating! But try not to be discouraged. Thinking strategically about assessment and instruction is a skill that takes professional development, coaching, and, as noted at the start of this chapter, a little trial and error. We aren't always going to get it right the first time around, even though that is always our intention.

Case 3: Student Example

Outcome Goal: By the middle of the year, Johnny will read 35 words correctly per minute on second-grade ORF passages, as a result of receiving a repeated-reading intervention three times a week.

Mrs. Hunter is a reading interventionist who supports second-graders. She noticed that Johnny scored low on ORF WC on the beginning-of-year screening. She attended a professional development workshop where she learned about the effectiveness of repeated-reading intervention for students who struggle to read fluently, and she decided to try it with Johnny. She set a goal for him to increase his ORF WC score by 25 points by the middle-of-year screening. She was disappointed when he didn't meet the goal, so she sought the support of her school psychologist. In working through the CIC steps, Mrs. Hunter realized that her hypothesis about Johnny needing a fluency intervention may have been off the mark. Investigation of the middle-of-year scores revealed that Johnny made too many errors while reading. The fluency intervention wasn't successful because it wasn't targeting the correct skill, which was accurate decoding. With the help of the school psychologist, Mrs. Hunter went back to the drawing board to do additional gap analysis and design a new intervention.

Case 4: Systems Example

Outcome Goal: By the middle of the year, 65 percent of the first graders will read nonwords correctly on a NWF assessment, without sounding them out.

At the beginning-of-year screening, only 35 percent of the first-grade students at Acme Elementary scored at or above benchmark on NWF. The first-grade teachers decided to seek support from the special education, EL, and gifted staff for assistance in teaching Tier 1 phonics and spelling in skill-based, teacher-led groups. They were disappointed to see that only 38 percent of the students met the NWF goals at the middle-of-year screening. When the team revisited their plan, they realized that while they had accomplished the goal of differentiating their ELA block, the program they were using was not explicit and systematic enough for the low-performing students. The first-grade team revised their plan for the second half of the year to include using their intervention program with students who scored below and well below benchmark.

YOU GOT LUCKY! Didn't Implement the Plan, Met the Goal

It is always a win when students wind up better readers. However, we feel better about that win when we know it was the result of our actions and not by accident. And remember, it's much easier to replicate success when we know what created that success. How can that happen if we don't carefully create and implement a plan?

Case 5: Student Example

Outcome Goal: By the middle of the year, Johnny will read 35 words correctly per minute on second-grade ORF passages, as a result of receiving a repeated-reading intervention three times a week.

Mrs. Hunter is a reading interventionist who supports second-graders. She noticed that Johnny scored low on ORF WC on the beginning-of-year screening. She attended a professional development workshop where she learned about the effectiveness of repeated-reading intervention for students who struggle to read fluently, and she decided to try it with Johnny. She reviewed his data and noticed that he met the ORF Accuracy goal but not the Words Correct goal, making him a perfect candidate for a repeated-reading intervention. She set a goal for him to increase his ORF WC score by 25 points by the middle-of-year screening. She was surprised and thrilled to see that he met the goal at the middle of year. However, she had to admit that she hadn't implemented the repeated-reading intervention as she had envisioned. She had a written plan, but her intervention sessions were so full that she never had time to implement it. With the help of the school psychologist, Mrs. Hunter went back to the plan and found time for the intervention.

Case 6: Systems Example

Outcome Goal: By the middle of the year, 65 percent of the first graders will read nonwords correctly on a NWF assessment, without sounding them out.

At the beginning-of-year screening, only 35 percent of the first-grade students at Acme Elementary scored at or above benchmark on NWF. The first-grade teachers decided to seek support from the special education, EL, and gifted staff for assistance in teaching Tier 1 phonics and spelling in skill-based, teacher-led groups. They were thrilled to see that 68 percent of the students met the NWF goals on the middle-of-year screening. However, when the team revisited their plan, they realized that they hadn't implemented the actions of differentiating their ELA block, using a program that was explicit and systematic enough for the low-performing students, and having an adult to teach each group. The first-grade team revised its plan for the second half of the year to include additional support for implementing the actions.

TIME TO BREAK DOWN BARRIERS!

Didn't Implement the Plan, Didn't Meet the Goal

Unfortunately, this fourth and final possible result of outcome assessment is common. Implementing a plan based on outcome assessment isn't easy, but it's essential given its potential positive impact on students. So we must keep that in mind as we go forward. We must keep our eye on that prize! Implementing action plans often means changing our own behavior, which is hard! We must build in the supports such as time, collaboration, professional development, and coaching that make it more likely for us to implement our plan.

Case 7: Student Example

Outcome Goal: By the middle of the year, Johnny will read 35 words correctly per minute on second-grade ORF passages, as a result of receiving a repeated-reading intervention three times a week.

Mrs. Hunter is a reading interventionist who supports second grade. She noticed that Johnny scored low on ORF WC on the beginning-of-year screening. She attended a professional development workshop where she learned about the effectiveness of repeated-reading intervention for students who struggle to read fluently, and she decided to try it with Johnny. She reviewed his data and noticed that he met the ORF Accuracy goal, but not the Words Correct goal, making him a perfect candidate for a repeated-reading intervention. She set a goal for him to increase his ORF WC score by 25 points by the middle-of-year screening. She was disappointed when he didn't meet the goal but had to admit that she hadn't implemented the repeated reading intervention as she had planned. She had a written plan, but the intervention sessions were so full that she never had time to implement it. With the help of the school psychologist, Mrs. Hunter went back to the plan and found time for the intervention.

Case 8: Systems Example

Outcome Goal: By the middle of the year, 65 percent of the first graders will read nonwords correctly on a NWF assessment, without sounding them out.

At the beginning-of-year screening, only 35 percent of the first-grade students at Acme Elementary scored at or above benchmark on NWF. The first-grade teachers decided to seek support from the special education, EL, and gifted staff for assistance in teaching Tier 1 phonics and spelling in skill-based, teacher-led groups. They were disappointed to see that only 38 percent of the students met the NWF goals at the middle-of-year screening. When the team revisited their plan, members realized that they hadn't implemented the actions of differentiating their ELA block, using a program that was explicit and systematic enough for the low-performing students, and having an adult to teach each group. The first-grade team revised their plan for the second half of the year to include additional support for implementing the actions as written.

We hope these case examples help you see how student outcome data and adult implementation data work together to arrive at an answer to Step 4 of the CIC: Did the plan work? We also hope they help you and your team establish conditions for implementing your plans and achieving results for your students.

Surviving the Implementation Dip

Thinking strategically about plans and carrying them out as designed doesn't come easily to many educators. And it's not the way most of us were taught in our training programs!

It can be hard to change the way we operate, and reading improvement is not always a linear path upward. But, when we hit bumps along the way, we are more likely to stay the course if we and our colleagues set realistic expectations. Here are some strategies for keeping the momentum going:

- Stay focused on student outcomes. If students aren't learning, change the way you teach.
- Engage all stakeholders in making key decisions.
- Avoid being distracted by new initiatives that seem like quick fixes.
- Celebrate even the smallest successes.
- Don't be afraid to admit you don't know the answer and need support.

To inspire you, we close this chapter with examples of results from real schools. It doesn't have to take years to see improvement. But it does take using assessments to know what your students need to learn, continually monitoring their progress and adjusting instruction, and focusing on outcomes.

If these schools can do it, you can, too!

	Percent at Benchmark Goal	
	Beginning of Year	End of Year
School A	39%	81%
School B	38%	85%
School C	28%	88%
School D	39%	85%
School E	59%	83%
School F	47%	84%
School G	16%	51%
School H	0%	81%

In Closing, Remember...

Outcome assessments provide information about the effectiveness of our instruction. They offer input about the extent to which our action plans were implemented and the effectiveness of those plans. It may be necessary to revisit or revise those plans when outcome assessments reveal that, although we implemented, they didn't help to resolve the problem. Dramatic improvement is possible through use of assessments in the CIC. Positive outcomes are attainable for your students, too!

In Chapter 8, we share how you can take all of this valuable assessment information and use it to inform your instruction… because as we keep saying, there's no point in collecting the data if you're not going to use it!

CHAPTER 8

Using Assessment Data to Inform Instruction

Now that you've collected information about your students, how can you most efficiently decide next steps? As you learned in Chapter 3, the Collaborative Improvement Cycle (CIC) helps you connect what you teach with what your students need. The hypothesis you generate in Step 2 of the cycle guides your instructional planning. As you learned in Chapter 6, we use ongoing progress-monitoring data to refine and intensify instructional support.

If you don't link assessment to instruction and intervention, you can all too easily get caught up in learning about new teaching strategies that may or may not meet your students' needs.

Here's an example: When Stephanie first learned about repeated reading for improving text reading fluency, she was so impressed with the results and shared her excitement with the teachers in her school. Before long, every student was getting repeated reading, whether they needed it or not! Similarly, after learning about the value of retelling, Kate found an elaborate cut-and-paste sequencing activity based on a book she read aloud, which ended up taking the entire period for her students to complete. (Fine-motor work in kindergarten is valuable, but not when it eats up precious minutes of literacy instruction.) These were tough lessons in connecting what students need to how Stephanie and Kate spent time during the school day.

We can avoid wasting time and increase the likelihood of providing effective instruction when we learn the proven practices found in the research. After all, our most vulnerable students don't have a minute to waste!

Effective Literacy Instruction

Decades of research confirms that direct, explicit instruction in essential skill areas is the most effective and efficient way to teach students to read and write (Mayer, 2004; Moreno, 2004). Explicit instruction works best for all (even your high-performing students) when they are learning something new or something they struggle with, so don't reserve it just for English learners and students with disabilities. Dr. Anita Archer summarizes that research and its instructional implications well in her book with Dr. Charles Hughes, *Explicit Instruction: Effective and Efficient Teaching* (2010).

Elements of Direct, Explicit Instruction

	Element	Description
1	**Focus instruction on critical content.**	In the context of a core, supplemental, or intervention reading curriculum review, the emphasis needs to be on phonemic awareness, phonics, fluency, vocabulary, and comprehension since these skills are predictive of reading outcomes.
2	**Sequence skills logically.**	Teach easier skills before more difficult skills. Note the way in which foundational skills are used in more complex tasks. Prioritize the teaching of high-utility skills (skills used more frequently) over less frequently used skills. Ensure there are opportunities for students to master prerequisite skills before teaching the skill itself. For example, teaching students to accurately produce the sounds /a/, /m/, /s/, and have them practice blending two of those sounds together before having them blend a consonant-vowel-consonant (CVC) word. Separate skills and strategies that are similar and might be confusing to students. For example, separate the teaching of /i/ and /e/ since those sounds are difficult for students to distinguish.
3	**Break down complex skills and strategies into smaller instructional units.**	Teach in small steps. Segmenting complex skills into smaller instructional units of new material reduces cognitive overload, processing demands, and working memory. Once the skills are mastered, they are practiced as a whole. For example, A Phonics Decoding Learning Progression: • Associating letters and sounds. • Blending sounds into words. • Reading words to build fluency. • Segmenting and spelling words. • Reading decodable text containing words with letter/sound associations.

Elements of Direct, Explicit Instruction (cont.)

	Element	Description
4	**Design lessons that are organized and focused.**	Lessons are on-topic, well-sequenced, and avoid digressions. For example, additional stories or examples that are not relevant to the skills that might take student's attention away from the learning.
5	**Begin lessons with a clear statement of the goals and your expectations.**	Teachers communicate what is to be learned and why it is important.
6	**Review prior skills and knowledge before beginning instruction.**	Provide a review of relevant information. Verify students have the prerequisite skills and knowledge to learn the skill being taught in the lesson. For example, before introducing students to the decodable reader, there is a pre-correct provided to the teacher stating the students must be able to read specific words before they begin to read those words in connected text. An instructional routine is provided that leads the students in practicing reading the target words.
7	**Provide step-by-step demonstrations.**	Model the skill. For example, clarify the decision-making processes needed to complete a task or procedure by engaging in a "think aloud" as the teacher performs the skill. Clearly demonstrate the target skill to show students' proficient performance.
8	**Use clear and concise language.**	Use consistent, unambiguous wording and terminology. For example, "Let's practice saying the sounds in the words that we will be reading. Look at the letters in Line 1. Say the sounds /ssss/, /mmm/, /aaa/, /t/".
9	**Provide an adequate range of examples and non-examples.**	Examples and non-examples allow the teacher to establish the boundaries of when and when not to apply a skill, strategy, concept, or rule. A wide range of examples are necessary. Presenting non-examples reduces the possibility a student will use the skill inappropriately. For example: Learning *a_e* and applying the rule of *e* making the letter *a* say its name requires many examples of *a_e* words but also should include words without *e* at the end. Students will know to distinguish when *a* says its name versus its sound.
10	**Provide guided and supported practice.**	Practice opportunities during the lesson build student confidence. The teacher needs to regulate the difficulty of the practice opportunities and guide them in demonstrating the skill. When students demonstrate success, the skill difficulty increases and teacher guidance decreases.

Elements of Direct, Explicit Instruction (cont.)

	Element	Description
11	**Require frequent responses.**	Have students respond frequently using the following verbal responses examples. • **Choral:** Use when answers are the same; focusing on recall and rehearsal of sounds/words, etc.; quick review of information • **Partners:** Use when responding to a question or a task; opportunity to have students teaching information to a partner (rapid reading of new words students just read); studying with a partner • **Individual:** Least desirable practice but there are times to make this a more acceptable practice (ask question and have students share answers with partners first before calling on individual students to provide the answer or ask question first and then call on individual students) • **Discussion:** Provide a well-designed question or prompt and have students discuss the answers. Sentence stems can be provided to scaffold student responses.
12	**Monitor student performance closely.**	Carefully watch and listen to students' responses so the teacher can verify their level of understanding of the information. Provide opportunities for students to elaborate on their responses and for the teacher to check understanding.
13	**Provide immediate affirmative and corrective feedback.**	Follow-up on students' responses as quickly as possible. Immediate feedback to students about the accuracy of their responses helps ensure high rates of success and reduces the likelihood of practicing errors. For example, correct sound errors with a sequence such as: • **Model (I do it):** Tell students the correct response "That sound is /aaa/." • **Test (You do it):** Have students repeat the correct response "What sound?" • **Delayed Test:** Test the item/skill that was incorrect at a later time in the lesson
14	**Deliver the lesson at a brisk pace.**	Use a rate of presentation that is brisk but includes a reasonable amount of time for processing, especially when they are learning new material. The desired pace is neither so slow that students get bored nor so quick that they cannot keep up.
15	**Help students organize knowledge.**	Because students struggle to see how some skills and concepts fit together, it is important to use teaching techniques that make the connections more apparent. Well-organized and connected information makes it easier for students to retrieve information and facilitate the information with new material.
16	**Provide distributed and cumulative practice.**	**Distributed practice** refers to multiple opportunities to practice a skill over time. **Cumulative practice** is a way to provide distributed practice by including practice opportunities that address both previously and newly acquired skills. Provide students with multiple practice attempts to help information move from short-term memory to long-term memory.

(Adapted from Archer & Hughes, 2010)

Applying Archer's key elements doesn't have to be complicated. For example, increasing the number of student responses per minute has been associated with increased learning (Gunter et al., 2004; MacSuga-Gage & Simonsen, 2015; Martin et al., 2018; Moore Partin et al., 2010; Sutherland & Wehby, 2001). Kate can vouch for the power of that. Going from "hands-up" model ("Who knows the sound for this digraph?") to a choral-response model ("Everyone, read this digraph.") has been a game-changer in terms of providing students with opportunities to respond. After all, it makes sense for the one doing the thinking, talking, and writing to be the one doing the learning!

Recommended Rates of Opportunities to Respond

Setting	Rate
Large group	3–6 opportunities per minute on average
Small group	8–12 opportunities per minute on average
New material	4–6 opportunities per minute with at least 80 percent accuracy
Review material	8–12 opportunities per minute with at least 90 percent accuracy
Students with intensive needs or disabilities	10 opportunities per minute on average

With this in mind, we turn to connecting assessment to instruction. Two big ideas frame our thinking:

1. Target instruction to where the student is on the instructional hierarchy, which is explained in Chapter 1 and revisited later in this chapter.
2. Target instruction to the lowest skill the student needs to learn, which we explain next.

Target the Lowest Skill Gap

Students learn fastest when instruction is focused on what the student needs to learn next—not something they already know and not a skill they don't have the prerequisites to learn yet.

The flowchart on the next page provides guidance for finding the lowest skill the student needs to learn. If you work with students in kindergarten and first grade, start at the bottom of the chart and work up until the student scores below benchmark, indicating he needs to learn that skill. If you work with students in second grade or higher, start from the top and work down. The questions on the left align with Steps 1 and 2 of the Collaborative Improvement Cycle: What is the gap between actual and desired outcomes? Why is the gap happening? The circles on the left suggest screening measures that will help you answer each question. Suggestions for instruction are on the right side and expanded upon in the rest of the chapter.

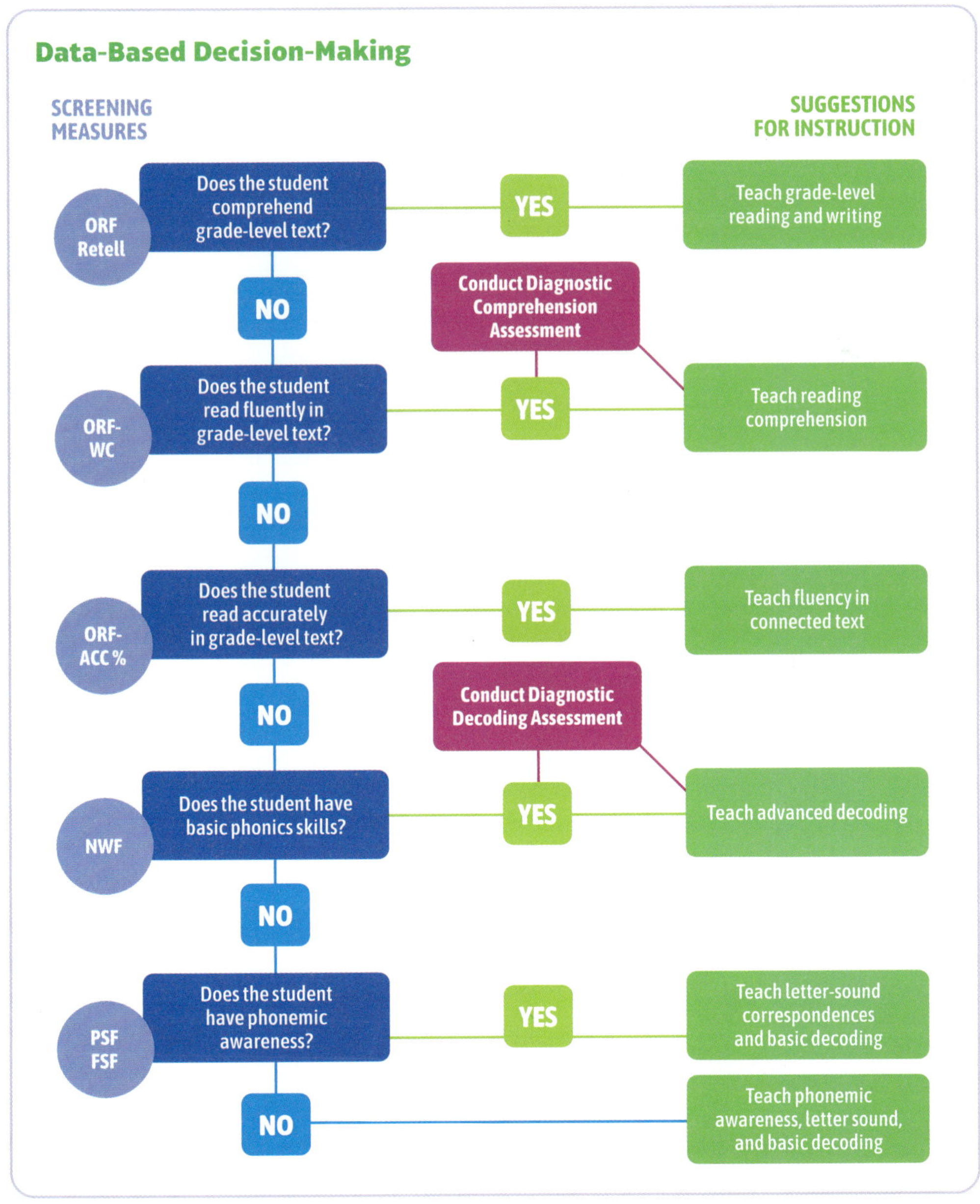

The chart below expands on the skill areas in the rectangles on the right of the flowchart. Column 1 shows general patterns of screening data. "Okay" means the student scored at or above expectation on the assessment, and "Low" means the student scored below or well below expectation on it. Column 2 explains what the pattern means—or, more specifically, what the student knows and needs to learn. And column 3 explains the type of instruction that might be helpful.

Read case studies based on the patterns in this chart here.

Common Score Patterns and Next Steps With Phoneme Segmentation Fluency (PSF)

Pattern	What It Means	What to Do Next
Okay First Sound Fluency (FSF) **Low PSF**	The student can isolate the beginning sound or sounds but is not segmenting the vowel from the ending sound.	Teach the student to separate the vowel sound from the ending sound. Use blocks or other manipulatives and letters. Be sure the student understands concepts such as first, middle, and last, and letter, sound, and word. Use activities for teaching phonemic awareness, such as those in *Making Words Stick*, pages 58–62.
Okay PSF	The student is segmenting sounds in words.	Check to be sure the student segmented *all* of the sounds in the words.

Common Score Patterns and Next Steps With Nonsense Word Fluency (NWF)

Pattern	What It Means	What to Do Next
Low NWF Correct Letter Sounds (CLS) **Low NWF Whole Words Read (WWR)**	• The student may be inaccurate and/or too slow with matching sounds to letters. • The student may have difficulty blending letter sounds to read words.	• Check PSF. • Teach letter-sound correspondence and how to blend letter sounds to read real VC and CVC words using routines such as those in *Rock Your Literacy Block* on pages 48–50.
Low NWF CLS **Okay NWF WWR**	• This is an unusual pattern. Open the booklet or pull up the probe details to see what errors the student made.	• Determine whether the student was accurate but slow with letter sounds, build fluency with letter sounds. • Determine whether the student made errors on letter sounds, teach letter-sound correspondence.

Common Score Patterns and Next Steps With Nonsense Word Fluency (NWF) (cont.)

Pattern	What It Means	What to Do Next
Okay NWF CLS **Low NWF WWR**	The student knows letter-sound correspondence but may have difficulty blending letter sounds to read words.	• Teach how to blend letter sounds to read real VC and CVC words using the routines in *7 Mighty Moves*, pages 71–76. • It may be helpful to start with real words that begin with letters that represent continuant sounds (e.g., /s/, /m/), limiting instruction to the letter-sound combinations the student is automatic with, and to teach and then remove a scaffold for reading words (point to each letter, say/whisper/think about the sound, say the word).
Okay NWF CLS **Okay NWF WWR**	The student knows letter-sound correspondence and can record words.	• Check to be sure the student can read the words without going sound by sound first. This will be marked with a single continuous underline under the letters and no other underlines. • If the student still needs to go sound by sound before reading the whole word, explicitly teach him or her to remove the scaffold for reading words (point to each letter, say/whisper/think about the sound, say the word). • Once the student can look at the word and read it without going sound by sound first, move on to the next pattern in your phonics scope and sequence (CCVC, CVCC, CVCe, etc.) such as the ones described in *7 Mighty Moves* on pages 44–47.

Common Score Patterns and Next Steps With Oral Reading Fluency (ORF)

Pattern	What It Means	What to Do Next
Low ORF Accuracy **Low ORF Words Correct (WC)** **Low ORF Retell**	The student may be having difficulty understanding text because he or she is reading too slowly and making too many errors.	• Give a diagnostic decoding assessment. • Consider testing back with Survey Level Assessment. • Teach the lowest phonics pattern the student hasn't yet mastered, practice in decodable text, using a routine such as the one in *7 Mighty Moves*, page 29. • Build language comprehension through questioning during read-alouds using the suggestions provided in *Strive for Five Conversations*, pages 90–91.
Okay ORF Accuracy **Okay ORF WC** **Low ORF Retell**	The student is an accurate and fluent reader but may be having difficulty with language comprehension and/or reading comprehension.	• Check language comprehension (vocabulary, syntax, morphology, text structure) with a language comprehension diagnostic and consider related instructional strategies such as those found in *Big Words For Young Readers*. • Use a comprehension intervention, such as paragraph shrinking, described in *7 Mighty Moves*, pages 149–150. • See the next page for more on teaching vocabulary.

Common Score Patterns and Next Steps With Oral Reading Fluency (ORF) (cont.)

Pattern	What It Means	What to Do Next
Okay ORF Accuracy **Low ORF WC** **Low ORF Retell**	The student can read accurately but not fluently, which may be impacting reading comprehension.	Build reading fluency with repeated reading, as described in *7 Mighty Moves* on pages 125–127.
Okay ORF Accuracy **Okay ORF WC** **Okay ORF Retell**	The student is reading grade-level text accurately, fluently, and for meaning.	Teach grade-level reading (see *Know Better, Do Better: Comprehension* for ideas) and writing.

Teaching Tiers of Vocabulary

We've been referring to the three tiers of instruction that make up MTSS throughout this book, and there are also three tiers of vocabulary (based on the work of Beck and colleagues, 2013) which are very different. See the image below for definitions and examples of each tier.

We often hear that it's most important to teach students high-utility "Tier 2" vocabulary words, but it's important to note that students who are English learners need explicit instruction in Tier 1 vocabulary as well.

"We absolutely want to focus on Tier 2 words, and they'll learn Tier 3 words specific to content areas," says Elsa Cárdenas-Hagan (personal communication, April 18, 2025), "but what we find with English Learners is oftentimes they don't know those Tier 1 words, and they may also have multiple meanings: the student might know what it means to run, but not what 'make a run to the store' or 'run your mouth' or 'they had a good run at the tournament' mean."

Explicit vocabulary instruction of even Tier 1 words is essential for ELs, and we can include strategies such as teaching idioms, expressions, and various meanings of words, drawing on cognates (English words that are the same or similar in the student's home language), as well as giving students extra opportunities to practice using these words in their speaking and writing, which will further support their language acquisition.

TIER 3:
content-specific, specialized words
(e.g., *photosynthesis, quadrilateral, sonata*)

TIER 2:
high-frequency words used across disciplines
(e.g., *emerge, factor, sinister*)

TIER 1:
basic, everyday words
(e.g., *table, run, cold*)

Fine-Tuning the Links Between Assessment and Instruction

While the chart on pages 128 to 130 illustrates how scores on screening, such as Acadience Reading and DIBELS 8th Edition, can be used to target instruction, they can be used to glean even more information. Pulling up the probe details or opening the paper-scoring booklet lets you move beyond the score to see exactly what the student knows and needs to learn next.

The chart below contains examples of common response patterns on each measure and their implications for instruction.

Common Response Patterns and Next Steps With Phoneme Segmentation Fluency (PSF)

Pattern	What It Means	What to Do Next
cave /k/ /ai/ /v/	The student can isolate beginning sounds in spoken words.	Teach segmenting the middle and ending sounds.
cave /k/ /ai/ /v/	The student can segment all sounds in spoken words.	Teach decoding and spelling.

Common Response Patterns and Next Steps With Nonsense Word Fluency (NWF)

Pattern	What It Means	What to Do Next
r u s	The student is making errors on letter sounds.	Teach accurate letter-sound connections through decoding and encoding real words.
r u s	The student is accurate with letter sounds but is not blending.	Teach the student to say each sound, then read the word. Then teach the student to fade the sound-by-sound blending and just read the word.
r u s	The student is reading sound by sound and then blending.	Teach the student to fade the sound-by-sound blending and just read the word.
r u s	The student is accurate with letter sounds and can blend automatically.	Teach the student to read words with patterns beyond CVC.

Common Response Patterns and Next Steps With Oral Reading Fluency (ORF)

Pattern	What It Means	What to Do Next
A Jump Rope Contest 0 It was the day of the jump rope contest. Kim and Anna were going 14 14 to compete. Kim was going to do a new trick. Anna was going to help. 29 29 The two girls watched as younger children took a turn in the contest. 42	The student is making too many errors to understand the text.	Administer NWF and review scores. If the student doesn't automatically read the words, see NWF patterns on the previous page. If the student can read VC and CVC words automatically, give a decoding diagnostic to determine the next pattern to teach.
A Jump Rope Contest 0 It was the day of the jump rope contest. Kim and Anna were going 14 14 to compete. Kim was going to do a new trick. Anna was going to help. 29 29 The two girls watched as younger children took a turn in the contest. 42	The student is reading accurately but too slowly to understand the text.	Use repeated readings to improve text reading fluency.

Additional Support for Planning Instruction: Revisiting the Instructional Hierarchy

The instructional hierarchy that was introduced in Chapter 1 is a framework for thinking about all learning, including learning to read, from acquiring a new skill to mastering it, to ultimately applying it over time and across contexts. It is one of the most foundational concepts in cognitive science. However, most teachers are not even taught about the hierarchy, let alone how to use it to target instruction.

Think about any new skill you have recently learned–for example, knitting. You didn't set out, on day one, to make a sweater. You started by acquiring the foundational skills of knitting, such as how to hold the needles, how to read a pattern, and how to complete the stitches. Maybe you took on a scarf as a project. You devoted all of your cognitive energy to producing the stitches correctly. Through trial and error, as well as, with any luck, corrective feedback from a more expert knitter, you became adept at producing the stitches. Then, with lots of practice, you became so accurate and automatic at knitting that you didn't have to devote any cognitive energy to producing stitches. In fact, you could knit while watching TV, having a conversation, or sitting in a professional development session. Over time, you moved from knitting scarves, to hats and gloves, and ultimately to sweaters, and began using many types of needles and yarn. In other words, you could generalize and transfer your accurate and fluent knitting skills to more advanced applications. The same instructional sequence, or hierarchy, applies to learning to read.

Knowing where a student is in the instructional hierarchy makes your instruction even more targeted, efficient, and effective.

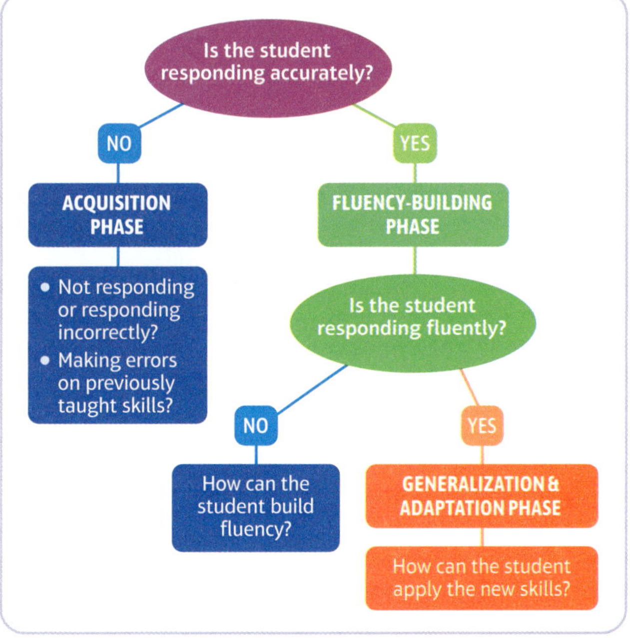

Errors, delayed responses, and inconsistent responses are indicators that a student is in the acquisition phase of the learning hierarchy. Students who are accurate but read slowly are in the fluency-building phase of the hierarchy. Students who are accurate and fluent are in the generalization and adaptation phase and are ready to apply their skills to solving problems and generalize them to new materials or settings. Without identifying the problem correctly, and positioning students in the appropriate phase of the instructional hierarchy, you run the risk of frustrating them by asking them to apply and generalize knowledge before it is solid.

When students are acquiring a skill, they need instruction and supported practice focused on that skill. Students who are in the acquisition phase should not focus on becoming faster. Fluency building happens after students are accurate.

What if we told you it was possible for two students to have the same score, but for different reasons? Wow! Laser-guided instruction! In the example below, both students earned 8 points on this row of NWF-CLS, but Javy needs instruction in blending letter sounds while Drew is ready to read patterns beyond CVC.

Student	Pattern	Instructional Focus
Javy	n i b h a n o m j e v	Blending letter sounds to read real words
Drew	n i b h a n o m j e v	Reading words with patterns beyond CVC

Your goal for students in the fluency-building phase should be automatic and independent responding. When students are accurate but slow, they need multiple practice opportunities to move to automaticity and independence. Students in the fluency-building phase shouldn't need any help to produce accurate responses. Because practice in this phase can be done independently or with partners, it is well-suited for literacy stations or centers. You can even teach students to check their own work.

Your goal for students in the generalization and adaptation phase is transfer of fluent skills to new contexts, flexible application of learned skills to new tasks, and use of those skills to solve complex problems. Students in this phase should be ready for independent work, partner work, problem-based learning, and challenge opportunities.

Phase in the Hierarchy	What You Will Observe	How It Might Look	What to Teach
Acquisition	• Errors • No response • Delayed response	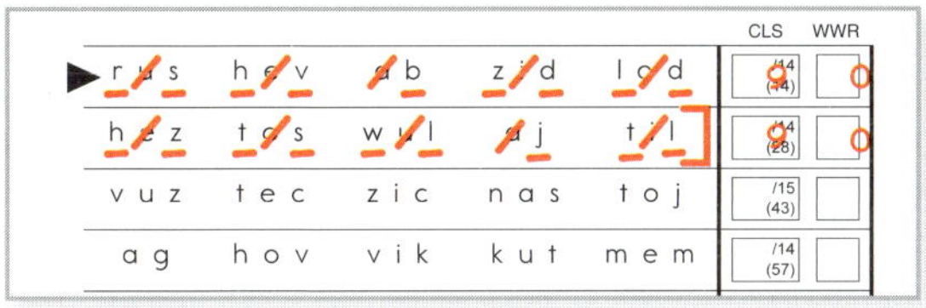 CLS WWR rus hev ab zid lod — 9 /14 (14) — 0 hez tos wul aj til — 9 /14 (28) — 0 vuz tec zic nas toj — /15 (43) ag hov vik kut mem — /14 (57)	• Correct letter-sound correspondences • Build accuracy
Fluency Building	• Accurate but slow and effortful response • Inconsistent response	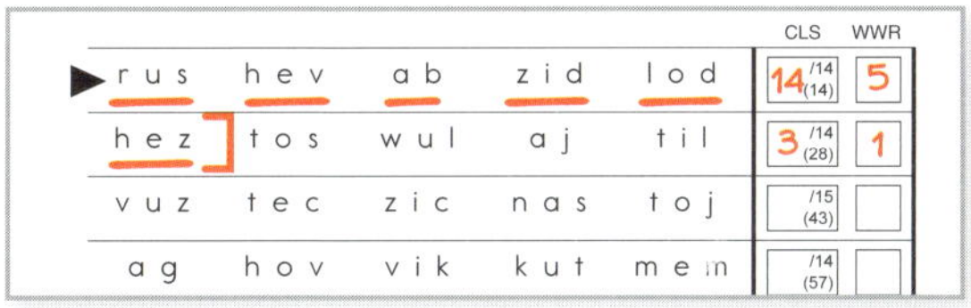 CLS WWR rus hev ab zid lod — 14 /14 (14) — 5 hez tos wul aj til — 3 /14 (28) — 1 vuz tec zic nas toj — /15 (43) ag hov vik kut mem — /14 (57)	• Automatic responding • Build fluency
Generalization and Adaptation	• Accurate and automatic response	 CLS WWR rus hev ab zid lod — 14 /14 (14) — 5 hez tos wul aj til — 14 /14 (28) — 5 vuz tec zic nas toj — 15 /15 (43) — 5 ag hov vik kut mem — 1 /14 (57) — 0 ek yun rab tif fov — /14 (71) puf zaj nib poj vel — /15 (86)	• Application of the skill in new settings, using new materials, or to more complex tasks • Plan for generalization, adaptation and transfer

Forming Targeted, Flexible, Skill-Based Groups

Now that you have screening and diagnostic assessment data to pinpoint what your students need, you can be much more targeted with your instruction. This deep information allows you to plan and deliver whole-group and small-group instruction that is both efficient and effective.

The chart below illustrates how middle-of-year screening data for Mrs. Smith's first-grade class might be used to inform instruction and grouping. A checkmark indicates scoring at or above benchmark. At this point in time, all students should score at or above benchmark on both NWF and ORF scores.

While Tim, Tony, Annie, Bobby, Bonnie, Donnie, and David have met the goals for basic decoding, text-reading accuracy, fluency, and comprehension, the rest of the students have not. Mrs. Smith will need to take that into consideration during whole-group instruction. She might do this by carefully pairing students for partner practice, providing some students with extra turns during cold calls, adding an extra example during modeling, or scaffolding a correct response with additional prompts. She also may want to provide small-group support to Carrie, Frank, and Fern to build their text-reading fluency, and to Greg and Ginger who need help reading patterns beyond CVC. She will also look for opportunities to give extra TLC to Henry who is not yet reading CVC words.

Mrs. Smith's Class

Name	ORF-WC	ORF-ACC	NWF-WWR	NWF-CLS
Tim	✔	✔	✔	✔
Tony	✔	✔	✔	✔
Annie	✔	✔	✔	✔
Bobby	✔	✔	✔	✔
Bonnie	✔	✔	✔	✔
Donnie	✔	✔	✔	✔
David	✔	✔	✔	✔
Carrie		✔	✔	✔
Frank		✔	✔	✔
Fern		✔	✔	✔
Greg			✔	✔
Ginger			✔	✔
Henry				✔

In some classrooms, it works well to provide whole-group instruction and then small-group support to pre-teach or reteach skills to struggling students. Some of the students also may get additional intervention support outside the classroom. This may be all that is needed to close the gap and get all students to the benchmarks, especially in kindergarten and first grade. You'll know if Tier 1 is effective if 80 percent or more of the students reach benchmark goals by the end of the year.

For example, at her small school, where there is often just one kindergarten class and students at similar skill levels, this approach has worked well for Kate. Since she started taking a structured literacy approach in 2022, at least 80 percent of her students have been at benchmark at the end of each year, so she feels confident continuing with whole-class followed by small-group instruction.

Also, Kate can easily scaffold instruction because the gaps are so small in her kindergarten class. For example, during a whole-class lesson in which her students engage in word chaining with magnetic letters, most of them immediately begin forming a word after it's dictated, whereas a few need prompts ("What sound does *wig* start with? What picture on the sound wall starts with /w/? Yes, *wagon*—so there's the letter you need!"). Scaffolding and choral responding allow all students to participate in routines and get what they need to move forward. This is different from thinking a student with no phonemic awareness or letter-sound knowledge can learn those skills through "exposure" while sitting through a second-grade phonics lesson.

In other classrooms or schools, the needs may be different, calling for a different approach. In schools that implement MTSS, grade-level team meetings center around the percentage of students who meet goals during screening across the year. If you start the year with more than 20 percent of the grade scoring below expectation, and the current way of delivering Tier 1 instruction hasn't gotten the vast majority of students to end-of-year benchmark goals in the past, it might be time to consider a different approach.

Mrs. Jones's Class

Name	ORF-WC	ORF-ACC	NWF-WWR	NWF-CLS
Tina	✔	✔	✔	✔
Terry	✔	✔	✔	✔
Ada	✔	✔	✔	✔
Darla	✔	✔	✔	✔
Debbie	✔	✔	✔	✔
Billy	✔	✔	✔	✔
Carl		✔	✔	✔
Connie		✔	✔	✔
Fay		✔	✔	✔
Farrah		✔	✔	✔
Gail			✔	✔
Hilary				✔

For example, what if Mrs. Jones taught in the same school as Mrs. Smith? The middle of first-grade screening data for Mrs. Jones are shown in the chart to the left.

Mrs. Smith and Mrs. Jones recognized the problems with each of them separately trying to support this diverse range of needs. For example, they each have just one student who struggles to read CVC words. It's hard to plan for a group of one!

Here are some additional concerns:

- Each teacher would be spending precious time teaching a whole-group lesson and then small-group lessons, not leaving much time in the day for the additional support that struggling readers need.
- They probably wouldn't be able to meet with each group every day, so some students (probably the strongest group) would not get targeted instruction from the teacher each day.
- If they met with more than one group, the rest of the students would be spending too much time without instruction from a teacher.
- The top students may become bored during lessons on skills they already know. The low-performing students may become frustrated sitting through instruction on skills for which they don't yet have the prerequisites.
- They would duplicate efforts if they both planned for four different groups in their classrooms.

Because the school uses MTSS, Mrs. Jones, Mrs. Smith, and all their colleagues who work with first-grade students, have a grade-level team meeting each week. This team includes the special education teacher and her educational assistant/paraprofessional, the reading interventionist, the gifted teacher and the EL teacher, and the principal. During the meeting, they reviewed the percentage of students who scored at benchmark on the middle-of-year screening. Almost half of the grade, 48 percent, was at risk of not reading for meaning at the end of the year. Last year, their middle-of-year results were slightly better, 52 percent, but the percent only increased to 65 percent by the end of last year. Since they wanted to significantly increase the percentage of students who met the benchmark at the end of the year, they decided to provide targeted, flexible, skill-based groups during the word recognition portion of Tier 1 instruction instead of whole-class instruction. Some of those educators (special education teacher, paraprofessional, reading interventionist, and EL teacher) met with the lowest-performing students at another time of day to provide a second dose of the same targeted instruction as Tier 2 or 3 intervention. This way, students would move faster through the scope and sequence and catch up by the end of the year.

The first-grade team used screening and diagnostic data to sort students into groups using the worksheet below.

Group	Students	ORF-WC	ORF-Accuracy	NWF-WWR	NWF-CLS	
1	Tom Tina Tony	✔	✔	✔	✔	Three students worked on decoding beyond CVC, reading fluency, and reading comprehension with the gifted teacher.
2 and 3	Terry Ada Bobby Darla Bonnie Debbie Billy Donnie Annie David	✔	✔	✔	✔	10 students worked on decoding beyond CVC, reading fluency, and reading comprehension. Five worked with Mrs. Smith. Five worked with the reading interventionist.
4 and 5	Carrie Fern Carl Fay Connie Farrah Frank		✔	✔	✔	Seven students worked on decoding beyond CVC and reading fluency. Four worked with Mrs. Jones. Three worked with the special education paraprofessional.
6	Greg Ginger Gail			✔	✔	Three students worked on decoding beyond CVC in word lists and text with the special education teacher.
7	Henry Hilary				✔	Two students worked on blending letter-sounds to read CVC words with the EL teacher.

Consider the initial grouping suggestions above as a starting point for forming groups. You can use information from diagnostic assessments, response patterns (including the instructional hierarchy), and additional knowledge about your students (such as who doesn't get along) to refine your grouping plan.

Learn more about forming groups with first-grade data from Stephanie here.

Don't Group Based on Composite Scores

You may have noticed that we didn't form groups based on how students scored on the Composite. While Composite Scores give us the best overall picture of a student's—and a system's—risk level, they're not all that helpful when it comes to instruction. If you form groups based on Composite Scores alone, you might wind up with students working on skills they already have, or miss out on targeting the skills they don't yet have. A better practice is to group based on scores on screening measures and diagnostic assessments.

Take the mid-year assessment results for kindergartners Anya, Marci, and Jack below. You might think Anya and Marci are fine because their Composite Scores are green (at benchmark), but Anya will need some support based on her score on Nonsense Word Fluency (NWF). Marci is doing well despite not knowing letter names, and may not need intervention, but that low LNF score is definitely something to keep an eye on. Jack's below benchmark Composite Score could lead you to presume he needs intervention in general, but his at-benchmark scores on FSF and PSF indicate his phonemic awareness is fine. His NWF score indicates that the alphabetic principle is the gap that needs to be closed.

	Letter Naming Fluency (LNF)	First Sound Fluency (FSF)	Phoneme Segmentation Fluency (PSF)	Nonsense Word Fluency Correct Letter Sounds (NWF-CLS)	Composite Score
Anya	high	at benchmark	at benchmark	below benchmark	at benchmark
Marci	really low	above benchmark	above benchmark	at benchmark	at benchmark
Jack	medium	at benchmark	at benchmark	well below benchmark	below benchmark

Lean Into Local Context

Your school may have more sections of each grade, different resource personnel, and a different percentage of on-track readers than the scenario we described earlier, but you can still apply the big ideas of MTSS:

- Design instruction and intervention based on student assessment data.
- Break down silos and use personnel flexibly to all support students.
- Meet as a team to review assessment data and plan instruction.
- Focus on prevention and early intervention through the primary way reading is taught to the class in the ELA block (Tier 1) and layer on extra doses of intervention as needed.
- If what you are doing is working to get all students to grade-level reading expectations, keep doing it.
- If what you are doing isn't working, thoughtfully consider what to change so you get a different result.

It may be particularly important to provide skill-based word recognition instruction, rather than whole-group instruction, in grades two and above, when the gap between high- and low-performing students is great and there are many students who score below expectation on screening. When schools try to respond to this reality with whole-group word recognition instruction in Tier 1 and targeted skill-based instruction in Tier 2 or 3, there just aren't enough minutes in the day to catch students up to grade level.

If the only way to meet students' needs is through intervention, the intervention system will quickly become overwhelmed. When the intervention system is overwhelmed, the interventions aren't effective at catching students up to grade-level performance. When the interventions aren't effective, lots of students will be referred for a special education evaluation, resulting in overwhelming the special education system or finding many students not eligible. This is a vicious cycle that many educators find themselves in when they start doing universal screening.

You can break the cycle by tracking the percent at benchmark on universal screening and using the data to build a tiered system of support that causes all students to be skilled readers, through prevention and early intervention. All it takes is one teacher sharing their concerns during a grade-level meeting, with their principal, or with a colleague. When a student is referred for intervention, it can be helpful to ask if any other students scored in the same way. This helps to avoid focusing on individual students when the instructional context needs to improve.

Remember, meeting students where they are with skill-based word recognition instruction in Tier 1 is only half of the equation. Students who are behind need a second dose of that instruction at another time of day as their Tier 2 or 3 intervention. This is how students move faster through the phonics and spelling scope and sequence and catch up to grade level. Also, keep in mind that all students still receive the language comprehension portion of Tier 1 instruction. This is when students are explicitly taught about morphology, syntax, vocabulary, listening comprehension, and content knowledge through engaging with complex text that is read to them until they have sufficient word recognition skills to read it themselves.

Using Progress Monitoring to Inform Instruction

All the hard work of determining what to teach—all the screening work and diagnostic work—should pay off in learning gains for your students. But you can't take that for granted! Ongoing progress monitoring tells you if the instructional plan you designed at Step 3 of the Collaborative Improvement Cycle is working. As you learned in Chapters 6 and 7, it's gratifying to see evidence of learning on a graph, based on progress monitoring. But what if you don't see that evidence? This section explains what you can do.

Researcher Jessica Toste led a master class for Stephanie's Reading Science Academy and shared some great insights about progress-monitoring data: "On the face of it, progress graphs seem simple: Here's a graph, now you'll make a decision... but graph comprehension studies in general, not just related to teachers and students, show that even very simple graphs are challenging for us, for humans, to read and interpret."

Dr. Toste shared the results of a research study she and her colleagues conducted with preservice teachers, delightfully titled "Graph Out Loud" (2025), which involved asking preservice teacher participants to indicate the next steps they would take based on progress-monitoring data, presented one data point at a time. If a participant indicated that he would make a change to instruction, he was asked to explain why.

Dr. Toste's study concluded that teachers need:

- More training (informed by both reading-science and the science of decision-making) and support when it comes to using progress-monitoring data (which is one of the reasons we wanted to write this book!)
- Hands-on practice with reading graphs and using real students' data
- Awareness of variation in real data. Participants frequently said they would make a change, based on even just one data point, but the rich information is in the trend. Generally, we want to consider at least four points to make an instructional decision as it's the trend over time that tells us the most, and Dr. Toste advises that we want to give ourselves as teachers—as well as our students—time to learn the instructional program before jumping to making a change.
- Flexibility to allow for the use of data-based decision rules, as well as room for teacher expertise and professional judgment when analyzing that data—but we don't want to go too far attributing student performance to "internal characteristics" of the student instead of instruction—the aspect we can control!

The chart below includes examples of progress-monitoring graphs and what they tell you about the most sensible instructional moves for students.

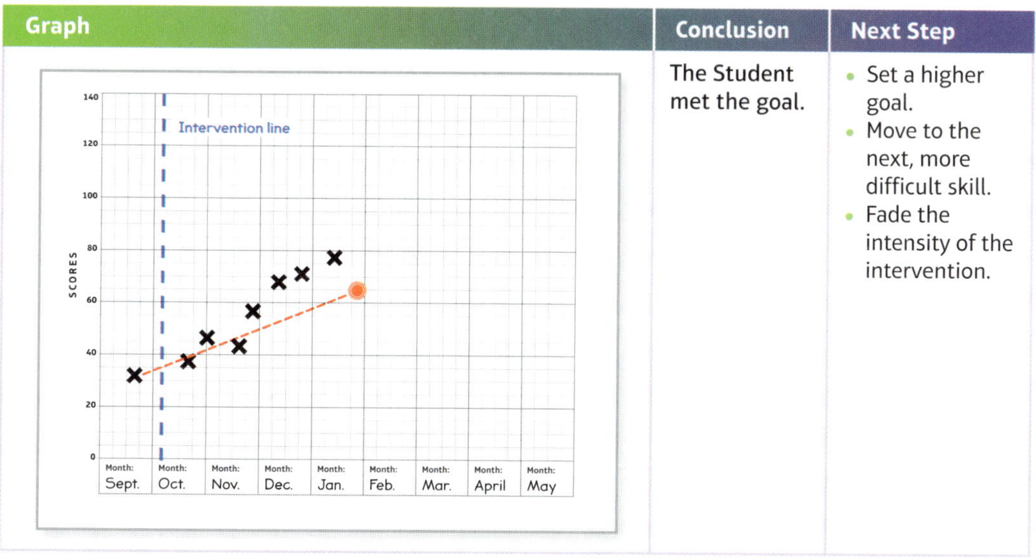

Graph	Conclusion	Next Step
	The Student met the goal.	• Set a higher goal. • Move to the next, more difficult skill. • Fade the intensity of the intervention.

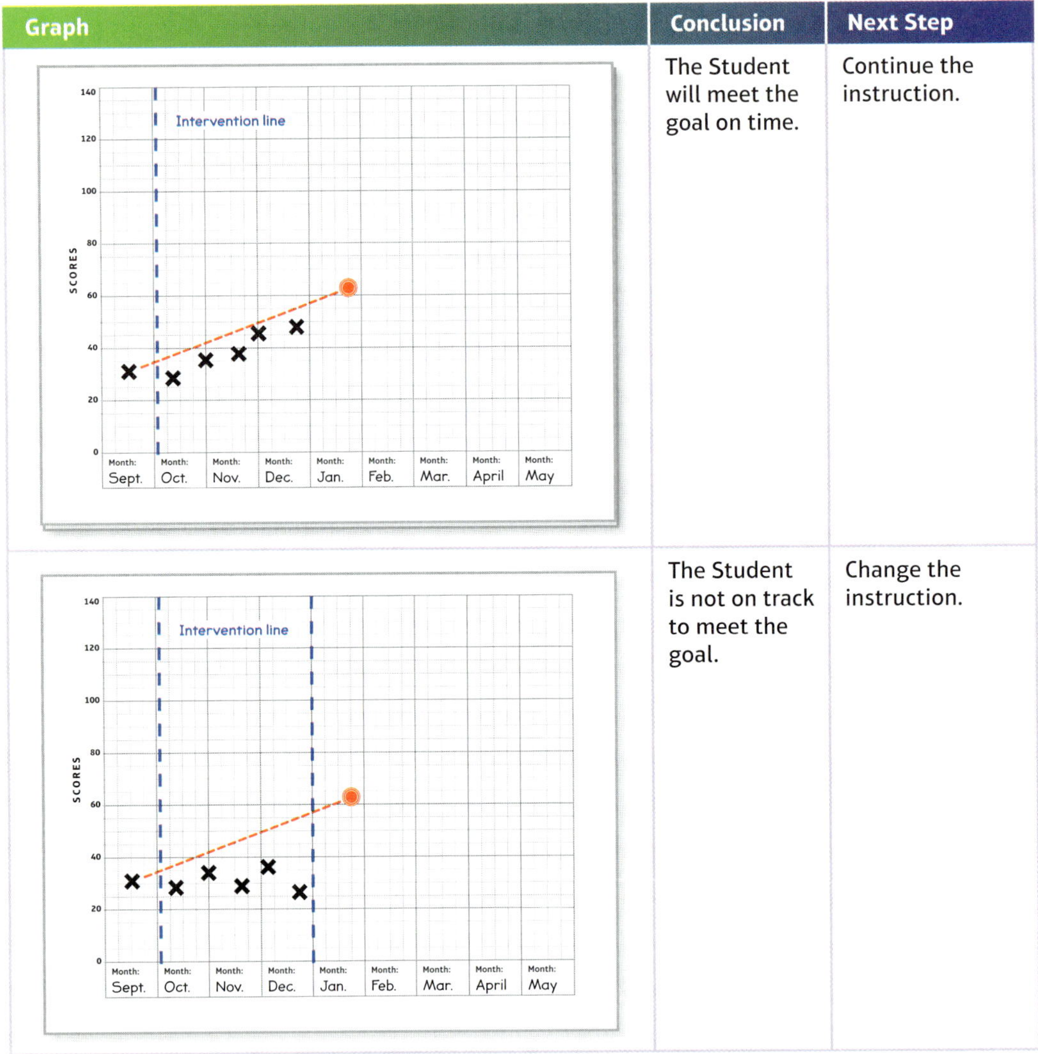

Graph	Conclusion	Next Step
	The Student will meet the goal on time.	Continue the instruction.
	The Student is not on track to meet the goal.	Change the instruction.

I Need to Make a Change... Now What?

When your data tell you that a change is in order, you might be tempted to switch to a different instructional program or intensify the intervention. But we caution you about making big changes unless they are absolutely necessary. The National Center on Intensive Intervention offers guidance on three broad categories to consider changing: instruction, curriculum, and environment (2024).

Working through the following questions will help you pinpoint exactly what to change. Remember that the more purposeful you are in thinking through the steps of the problem-solving process, the more likely you are to see success with the first plan you put in place.

Is the change needed because of instruction? Ask yourself:

- Is student attendance a concern?
  - If yes, can it be better supported?
- Is the intervention focused on the right skill for this student?
  - If no, determine the lowest essential skill the student hasn't yet mastered.
- Are evidence-based instructional materials, approaches, and programs being used?
- Was intervention delivered as planned (e.g., number of days per week, minutes per day?)
  - If yes, consider intensifying (more days per week, more minutes per day).
  - If no, consider how to ensure consistency of delivery (e.g., scheduling conflicts, interruptions).
- Was training and coaching provided to the interventionist?
  - If no, provide that support.

Burning Question

How can we track when interventions are changed?

When we change an element of an intervention, we add a vertical line to the graph to indicate the date when instruction changed. Doing that helps us see clearly the instruction that worked best for the student, and for how long the student has been receiving it.

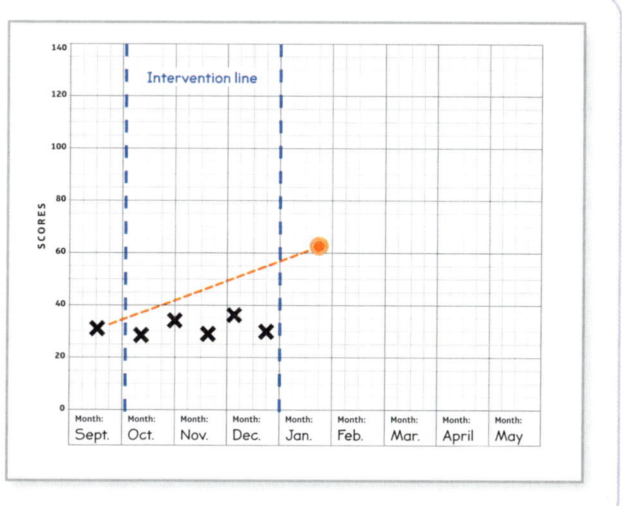

- Is the pace quick enough with ample opportunities to respond? (See chart on page 126, "Recommended Rates of Opportunities to Respond.")
    - If not enough opportunities to respond, consider reducing group size.
- Is there frequent corrective feedback?
    - If not, increase this.
- Are other students in the group making progress?
    - If yes, the adjustment may need to be made just for this child.
    - If no, make sure research-aligned instruction is targeting the lowest skill deficit.

Is the change needed because of curriculum? Ask yourself:

- Is there a clear scope and sequence?
- Is it the right level of difficulty? (Very low scores may mean that measurement level is too difficult and/or doesn't align with content of instruction—we want goals to be ambitious but realistic.)
- Is the right skill being addressed? (e.g., the small group is focused on phonics but the student still struggles with phonemic awareness?)
- Is the right area of the instructional hierarchy the focus? (e.g., we can't work on automaticity/rate in a skill before establishing accuracy)

Burning Question

How can we evaluate the effectiveness of Tier 2 and 3 interventions?

It is easy to get focused on individual students and lose sight of the big picture. When you see a student who isn't making sufficient progress, it is a good idea to look at the other students in the same small group. If no one is growing, the right response is to consider the effectiveness of the intervention. But if all but one student are growing (see Student 4), the right response is to analyze factors about that individual student that can be changed to accelerate growth.

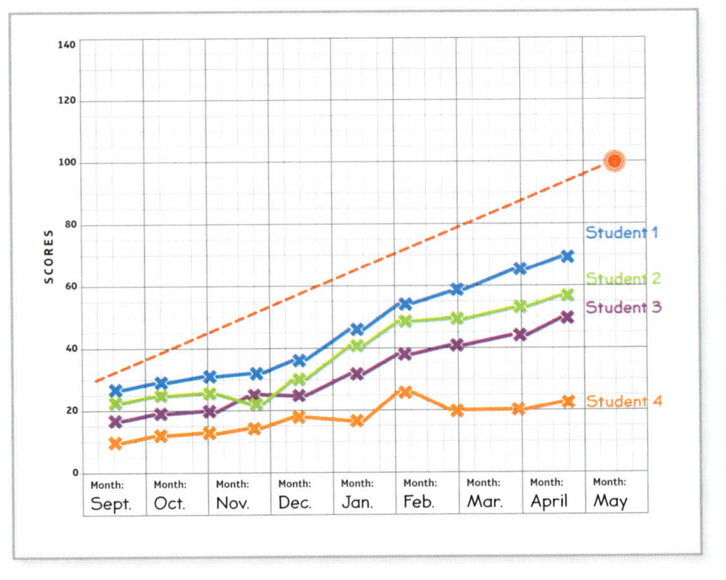

Is the change needed because of environment? Ask yourself:

- Are clear expectations for behavior during small-group time communicated to the students?
- Does the student seem distracted by the setting during instruction?
- Does the student seem unmotivated during instruction? (Motivation may contribute to highly variable assessment data.)
  - Is positive reinforcement being utilized?—more individualized incentives/motivation/encouragement

What if students are making progress in intervention but are having difficulty applying what they have learned in other settings?

Consider the instruction dimension: Can the students transfer/generalize what they're practicing?

Also, consider the environment dimension: Are you managing your classroom effectively? As the National Center on Intensive Intervention (2024) reminds us, "Teachers who use effective classroom management practices can expect a significant reduction of disruptive, inappropriate, or aggressive behavior from students."

Lastly, consider out-of-school factors. Calling a meeting with the student (if appropriate), family, and school support team could be beneficial for gathering student-specific information and additional context that can come from the student's home.

Should I Share Progress-Monitoring Data With Students?

Tracking their own data can be motivating to students, particularly those who are below benchmark. Hasbrouck and Glaser (2018) referred to a 1993 study by Fuchs, Fuchs, Hamlett, Walz, and Germann when they wrote, "Research indicates that students make better progress when they chart their own progress," so consider sharing progress-monitoring data with students while always remaining encouraging and supportive of students who are struggling readers and those with reading disabilities.

What Does It Mean to Intensify Support?

In Chapter 3, we described Tier 3 intervention as being "more intensive" than Tier 1 or 2 instruction. In this context, the word "intensive" means more time and resources are needed to plan and deliver the instruction. The following are characteristics of the Tier 3 system of support that make it more intensive than Tier 1 and 2.

- More explicit, supportive, and individualized instruction
- More time (more time each day, more days per week)
- More opportunities to respond and practice
- More training and coaching for the instructor
- More frequent progress monitoring

Tier 3 is not special education. Students with reading disabilities are served in all three tiers. Students do not have to be on Individualized Education Plans (IEP) to get Tier 3 intervention. Some students receiving Tier 3 intervention will never be on an IEP. Special education personnel, funding, and other resources can be used to support students who receive Tier 3 support, just as they can with any of the tiers.

Planning Tier 3 Intervention

One of the ways in which Tier 3 intervention is more intensive than Tier 2 is in terms of the people involved in planning. Tier 2 is planned by a grade-level team, but Tier 3 is planned by a team that forms for each individual student. Students who don't make sufficient progress in spite of receiving effective Tier 1 and 2 intervention need our best thinking. This is when we bring in the students' parents or guardians, community professionals who are working with the student, and all of the school personnel who are working with the student or who have expertise to help the student.

The student-level team engages in CIC to write an action plan that is customized for this student. This is ongoing work that may require multiple cycles through questions and assessments in the quest to enable learning. This is not about documenting failure. Be careful not to unintentionally incentivize lack of progress by using policies or paperwork that emphasize lack of growth.

Special Education Evaluations

In the United States and Canada, federal and state/provincial laws dictate policies and procedures requiring school districts to find, evaluate, and serve students with disabilities. The MTSS model outlined in this book is consistent with those laws. In fact, we would argue it supports schools to find and serve students with disabilities faster than the traditional refer-test-place approach that MTSS was created to replace.

Evaluations in the Traditional Model

MTSS was conceptualized as an alternative approach to identifying and serving students with disabilities due to the many flaws with the traditional refer-test-place approach. Before MTSS, teachers had to recognize a student was struggling with reading, refer to a team of their peers, wait for their decision, and hope the student got the support they needed. If a specific learning disability such as dyslexia was suspected, the evaluation that was part of that process typically involved giving an IQ test and an achievement test. If the student had a 30-point difference between their IQ and achievement test score, they were deemed to have a disability and an IEP was written. If there wasn't a 30-point discrepancy, they could not access the intensive intervention support available through special education services.

While it is beyond the scope of this book to detail the research on the flaws with the discrepancy model, it is important to mention the issues because, unfortunately, so many districts are still engaging in this outdated and discredited practice. First, as Dr. Jack Fletcher has said, "IQ is uncoupled from reading achievement." IQ is not a good predictor of reading ability or achievement. IQ testing does not inform instruction in any way or inform the level of support students need. Students with high IQ scores do not need different instruction than students with low IQ scores, and IQ scores don't distinguish who will make faster progress in learning to read. Additionally, discrepancies between IQ and achievement do not show up until around third grade, which is too late for providing intensive intervention. Low readers have the same instructional needs, whether or not they have a discrepancy. The time spent conducting IQ and achievement tests could be better spent on instruction.

Evaluations in the MTSS Model

MTSS was originally conceptualized as an alternative to the traditional approach to special education eligibility due to the research on prevention of reading difficulties, the advances in direct assessment of reading skills, and the need to integrate general education and special education service delivery. In MTSS, a student is suspected of having a reading disability, such as dyslexia, when the intervention that is required for that student to make progress is so intensive and individualized that it can't be maintained with general education resources. The specially designed instruction the student has been receiving is written into an IEP so the student has the legal right to that service going forward.

Evaluations Conducted by Outside Providers

In the United States, school districts are legally required to conduct evaluations when a teacher or parent/guardian suspects a disability. If families pay for an evaluation outside of the school district, the district has failed to communicate and/or execute their responsibilities. When a district receives the results of an outside evaluation, they can conduct their own evaluation or accept the results of the outside provider. The district must consider the results of an outside evaluation, but only the district can determine if a student has a disability and needs special education services through an IEP. Teachers and parents/guardians must understand that a dyslexia diagnosis from an outside provider does not obligate the district to provide special education services.

In Closing, Remember...

We collect assessment data to inform instruction. Questions about your students should determine the assessments you use. When those questions are framed within the Collaborative Improvement Cycle, it is easier to link specific information about students' needs to instruction and intervention. Your students will make faster progress when you target instruction to their skill needs, when you spend time each day focusing on those needs, and when you spend less time on skills they either already have or aren't ready to learn. You can address the needs of more students when you collaborate with colleagues to plan the tiers of instruction and intervention that reflect your school's resources, match your students' needs, and get all students to reach grade-level reading expectations.

Conclusion

Now that you're equipped with a thermometer (screener), x-ray (diagnostic), GPS (progress monitoring), and rearview mirror (outcome), we hope you have all the tools you need to be a more efficient and effective reading teacher. More importantly, we hope the Collaborative Improvement Cycle provides the framework for thinking about the connections among these tools, as you work in teams to improve results for each and every student. It is tempting for busy educators to jump to what may seem like easy or quick solutions without careful data analysis. The more you use the tools in this book, the more efficient you will become at planning and delivering effective reading instruction.

In the MTSS framework, universal screening data tell you which students are at risk, but also which instructional systems (Tier 1, 2, or 3) are at risk, so you can get the conditions right for all students to become skilled readers. Instructionally relevant diagnostic assessments provide precision for your next instructional moves. Ongoing progress-monitoring data help you change instruction when students aren't on track to reach their goals. The reflection offered by outcome assessments confirms that you've gotten students where they need to be.

Whether you are the only teacher in your school working to implement the science of reading, or part of a team of educators on this mission, we hope the terminology, techniques, and tools required for this transformation are now more accessible to you. What you've learned equips you with the knowledge and skills to make informed assessment selections, participate on teams at the board/district, school, and student levels, and dig underneath complex reading issues with targeted instruction and intervention.

Welcome to the world of assessment nerds! We are so happy you've joined us. We hope reading assessment will be the key that unlocks literacy for all your students, as it continues to be for both of us.

References

Acadience Learning. (2022). *Acadience Reading Diagnostic: Phonemic Awareness & Word Reading and Decoding (PA & WRD)*. Voyager Sopris Learning.

Al Otaiba, S., Folsom, J. S., Schatschneider, C., Wanzek, J., Greulich, L., Meadows, J., Li, Z., & Connor, C. M. (2011). Predicting first-grade reading performance from kindergarten response to tier 1 instruction. *Exceptional Children, 77*(4), 453–470.

Archer, A. L., & Hughes, C. A. (2010). *Explicit instruction: Effective and efficient teaching*. The Guilford Press.

Ball, C. R., & O'Connor, E. (2016). Predictive utility and classification accuracy of oral reading fluency and the Measures of Academic Progress for the Wisconsin Knowledge and Concepts Exam. *Assessment for Effective Intervention, 41*(4), 195–208.

Bao, X., Komesidou, R., & Hogan, T. P. (2024). A review of screeners to identify risk of developmental language disorder. *American Journal of Speech-Language Pathology, 33*(3), 1548–1571. https://doi.org/10.1044/2023_AJSLP-23-00286

Beck, I. L., McKeown, M. G., & Kucan, L. (2013). *Bringing words to life: Robust vocabulary instruction* (2nd ed.). The Guilford Press.

Brady, S. (2020, October). A 2020 perspective on research findings on alphabetics (phoneme awareness and phonics): Implications for instruction (expanded version). *The Reading League*. https://www.thereadingleague.org/wp-content/uploads/2020/10/Brady-Expanded-Version-of-Alphabetics-TRLJ.pdf

Brown, K. J., Patrick, K. C., Fields, M. K., & Craig, G. T. (2021). Phonological awareness materials in Utah kindergartens: A case study in the science of reading. *Reading Research Quarterly, 56*(S1), S249–S272.

Brown, S., & Stollar, S. (2025). *MTSS for reading improvement: A leader's tool kit for schoolwide success*. Solution Tree.

Burgess, S. R., & Lonigan, C. J. (1998). Bidirectional relations of phonological sensitivity and prereading abilities: Evidence from a preschool sample. *Journal of Experimental Child Psychology, 70*(2), 117–141.

Burns, M. K. (2023). Examining the learning hierarchy with accuracy and rate scores for reading fluency among second- and third-grade students. *Journal of Behavioral Education*.

Burns, M. K., Codding, R. S., Boice, C. H., & Lukito, G. (2010). Meta-analysis of acquisition and fluency math interventions with instructional and frustration level skills: Evidence for a skill-by-treatment interaction. *School Psychology Review, 39*(1), 69–83.

Burns, M. K., & Parker, D. C. (2014). *Curriculum-based assessment for instructional design: Using data to individualize instruction*. The Guilford Press.

Burns, M. K., Pulles, S. M., Maki, K. E., Kanive, R., Hodgson, J., Helman, L. A., McComas, J. J., & Preast, J. L. (2015). Accuracy of student performance while reading leveled books rated at their instructional level by a reading inventory. *Journal of School Psychology, 53*(6), 437–445.

Carta, J. J., & Young, R. M. (Eds.). (2019). *Multi-tiered systems of support for young children: Driving change in early education*. Paul H. Brookes Publishing Co.

Castillo, J. M., Wolgemuth, J. R., McKenna, M., Hite, R., & Latimer, J. D. (2024). A qualitative synthesis of research on professional learning for multi-tiered systems of support. *Teacher Education and Special Education, 47*(3), 203–224.

Castles, A., Rastle, K., & Nation, K. (2018). Ending the reading wars: Reading acquisition from novice to expert. *Psychological Science in the Public Interest, 19*(1), 5–51.

Castles, A., Wilson, K., & Coltheart, M. (2011). Early orthographic influences on phonemic awareness tasks: Evidence from a preschool training study. *Journal of Experimental Child Psychology, 108*(1), 203–210.

Clemens, N. H., Hagan-Burke, S., Luo, W., Cerda, C., Blakely, A., Frosch, J., Gamez-Patience, B., & Jones, M. (2015). The predictive validity of a computer-adaptive assessment of kindergarten and first-grade reading skills. *School Psychology Review, 44*(1), 76–97.

Clemens, N., Solari, E., Kearns, D. M., Fien, H., Nelson, N., Stelega, M., Burns, M., St. Martin, K., & Hoeft, F. (2021, December 14). They say you can do phonemic awareness instruction "in the dark," but should you? A critical evaluation of the trend toward advanced phonemic awareness training.

Consortium on Reading Excellence (CORE). (2008). *Assessing reading: Multiple measures, K–8*. Arena.

Curtis, M. J., & Stollar, S. (2002). System-level consultation and organizational change. In A. Thomas and J. Grimes (Eds.), *Best practices in school psychology IV* (pp. 51–58). National Association of School Psychologists.

Deno, S. L. (2002). Problem solving as "best practice." In A. Thomas & J. Grimes (Eds.), *Best practices in school psychology IV* (pp. 37–55). National Association of School Psychologists.

Deno, S. L., & Mirkin, P. K. (1977). *Data-based program modification: A manual.* Council for Exceptional Children.

Dowhower, S. L. (1991, April). *The beginning of the beginning: A comparison of classroom management practices of novice and experienced kindergarten teachers the first month of school* [Paper presentation]. Annual Meeting of the American Educational Research Association, Chicago, IL.

Education Quality and Accountability Office. (2023). *Assessment of reading, writing and mathematics*. https://www.eqao.com/the-assessments/

Ehri, L. C. (2020). The science of learning to read words: A case for systematic phonics instruction. *Reading Research Quarterly, 55*(S1), S45–S60.

Farrell, L., & Hunter, M. (2016). *Advanced decoding survey*. Really Great Reading. https://www.reallygreatreading.com/sites/default/files/2025-01/Really_Great_Reading_Advanced_Decoding_Survey_Plus_RGRADSPLUS021916.pdf

FastBridge Learning. (2019). *FastBridge Learning: Benchmarks and norms interpretation and use guidelines (version 4)*. FastBridge Learning.

Fien, H., Chard, D. J., & Baker, S. K. (2021). Can the evidence revolution and multi-tiered systems of support improve education equity and reading achievement? *Reading Research Quarterly, 56*(1), S105–S118.

Foorman, B. R., Francis, D. J., Fletcher, J. M., Schatschneider, C., & Mehta, P. (1998). Erratum: The role of instruction in learning to read: Preventing reading failure in at-risk children. *Journal of Educational Psychology, 90*(2), 235.

Foulin, J. N. (2005). Why is letter-name knowledge such a good predictor of learning to read? *Reading and Writing: An Interdisciplinary Journal, 18*(2), 129–155.

Francis, D. J., Shaywitz, S. E., Stuebing, K. K., Shaywitz, B. A., & Fletcher, J. M. (1996). Developmental lag versus deficit models of reading disability: A longitudinal, individual growth curves analysis. *Journal of Educational Psychology, 88*(1), 3–17.

Fuchs, L. S., Fuchs, D., Hamlett, C. L., Walz, L., et al. (1993). Formative evaluation of academic progress: How much growth can we expect? *School Psychology Review, 22*(1), 27–48.

Fuchs, L. S., Fuchs, D., Hosp, M. K., & Jenkins, J. R. (2001). Oral reading fluency as an indicator of reading competence: A theoretical, empirical, and historical analysis. *Scientific Studies of Reading, 5*(3), 239–256.

Glaser, D. R. (2023). *Morphemes for little ones*. 95 Percent Group. https://store.95percentgroup.com/morphemes-for-little-ones-teaching-tools-set

Good, R. H., III, Kaminski, R. A., Dewey, E. N., Wallin, J., & Powell-Smith, K. A. (2013, revised 2019). *Acadience Reading K–6 technical manual*. Acadience Learning Inc. https://acadiencelearning.org/wp-content/uploads/2020/01/Acadience_Reading_K-6_Technical_Manual.pdf

Good, R. H., III, Kaminski, R. A., Cummings, K. D., Dufour-Martel, C., Petersen, K., Powell-Smith, K. A., Stollar, S., & Wallin, J. (2020). *Acadience Reading K–6 Assessment Manual*. Acadience Learning Inc.

Good, R. H., III, & Kaminski, R. A. (1996). Assessment for instructional decisions: Toward a proactive/prevention model of decision-making for early literacy skills. *School Psychology Quarterly, 11*(4), 326–336.

Good, R. H., III, Kaminski, R. A., Fien, H., Powell-Smith, K. A., & Cummings, K. D. (2012). How progress monitoring research contributed to early intervention for and prevention of reading difficulty. In C. A. Espin, K. L. McMaster, S. Rose, & M. M. Wayman (Eds.), *A measure of success: The influence of curriculum-based measurement on education* (pp. 113–124). University of Minnesota Press.

Good, R. H., III, & Kaminski, R. A. (2020). *Acadience Reading K–6 Assessment Manual*. Acadience Learning Inc.

Gough, P. B., & Tunmer, W. E. (1986). Decoding, reading, and reading disability. *Remedial & Special Education, 7*(1), 6–10.

Gray, J. S., & Powell-Smith, K. A. (2025). Rapid automatized naming: What it is, what it is not, and why it matters. *Annals of Dyslexia, 75*(1), 1–18.

Gresham, F. M. (1989). Assessment of treatment integrity in school consultation and prereferral intervention. *School Psychology Review, 18*(1), 37–50.

Gresham, F. M. (2004). Current status and future directions of school-based behavioral interventions. *School Psychology Review, 33*(3), 326–343.

Gresham, F. M., MacMillan, D. L., Beebe-Frankenberger, M. E., & Bocian, K. M. (2000). Treatment integrity in learning disabilities intervention research: Do we really know how treatments are implemented? *Learning Disabilities Research & Practice, 15*(4), 198–205.

Gunter, P. L., Reffel, J. M., & Barnett, C. A. (2004). Academic response rates in elementary-school classrooms. *Education and Treatment of Children, 27*(2), 105–113.

Gutkin, T. B., & Curtis, M. J. (1990). School-based consultation: Theory, techniques, and research. In T. B. Gutkin & C. R. Reynolds (Eds.), *The handbook of school psychology* (2nd ed., pp. 577–611). John Wiley & Sons.

Hagermoser Sanetti, L. M., Chafouleas, S. M., Christ, T. J., & Gritter, K. L. (2009). Extending use of direct behavior rating beyond student assessment: Applications to treatment integrity assessment within a multi-tiered model of school-based intervention delivery. *Assessment for Effective Intervention, 34*(4), 251–258.

Haring, N. G., Lovitt, T. C., Eaton, M. D., & Hansen, C. L. (1978). *The fourth r: Research in the classroom*. Charles E. Merrill Publishing.

Harlacher, J. E., Collins, A., & Potter, J. (2024). *Untangling data-based decision making: A problem-solving model to enhance MTSS*. Marzano Resources.

Hasbrouck, J. E. (2024). Data-informed instruction. In N. Young & J. E. Hasbrouck (Eds.), *Climbing the ladder of reading and writing* (pp. 46–65). Benchmark Education.

Hasbrouck, J. E., & Glaser, D. R. (2018). *Reading fluency: Understand – assess – teach: Professional learning guide for leaders*. Benchmark Education.

Hasbrouck, J. E. (2006; 2011; 2017; 2025). *Quick phonics screener (QPS)*. Read Naturally.

Hosp, M. K., & Hosp, J. L. (2007). When the emerging alternative becomes the standard. In C. A. Espin, K. L. McMaster, S. Rose, and M. M. Wayman (Eds.), *A measure of success* (pp. 49–58). University of Minnesota Press.

Hoover, W. A., & Tunmer, W. E. (2021). The primacy of science in communicating advances in the science of reading. *Reading Research Quarterly, 57*(2), 399–408.

Hudson, J. (2005). Joint education summit focuses on disparities in nation's schools. *The Crisis, 112*(3), 60–61.

International Dyslexia Association. (2018). *Knowledge and practice standards for teachers of reading.* https://dyslexiaida.org/knowledge-and-practices/

International Dyslexia Association. (2022). *Building phoneme awareness: Know what matters.* https://dyslexiaida.org/building-phoneme-awareness-know-what-matters/

Joint Committee on Standards for Educational and Psychological Testing. (2014). *Standards for educational and psychological testing* (7th ed.). American Educational Research Association.

Juel, C. (1988). Learning to read and write: A longitudinal study of 54 children from first through fourth grades. *Journal of Educational Psychology, 80*(4), 437–447.

Kaminski, R. A., Abbott, M., Bravo Aguayo, K. B., & Good, R. H., III. (2023). *Preschool Early Literacy Indicators (PELI).* Acadience Learning Inc.

Kemeny, L. (2023). *7 mighty moves: Research-backed, classroom-tested strategies to ensure K-to-3 reading success.* Scholastic.

Kemeny, L. (2025). *Rock your literacy block: Mighty moves to organize your day and optimize student learning.* Scholastic.

Kuhn, M. R., & Stahl, S. A. (2000). *Fluency: A review of developmental and remedial practices* (CIERA Report No. 2-008). Office of Educational Research and Improvement.

Lane, H., & Contesse, V. (2022). *UFLI foundations: An explicit and systematic phonics program.* Ventris Learning.

Lerner, M. D., & Lonigan, C. J. (2016). Bidirectional relations between phonological awareness and letter knowledge in preschool revisited: A growth curve analysis of the relation between two code-related skills. *Journal of Experimental Child Psychology, 144*, 166–183.

MacSuga-Gage, A. S., & Simonsen, B. (2015). Examining the effects of teacher-directed opportunities to respond on student outcomes: A systematic review of the literature. *Education and Treatment of Children, 38*(2), 211–239.

Martin, B., Sargent, K., Van Camp, A., & Wright, J. (2018). *Intensive intervention practice guide: Increasing opportunities to respond as an intensive intervention.* Office of Special Education Programs, U.S. Department of Education.

Mayer, R. E. (2004). Should there be a three-strikes rule against pure discovery learning? The case for guided methods of instruction. *American Psychologist, 59*(1), 14–19.

Mesmer, H. A. (2024). *Big words for young readers: Teaching kids in grades K to 5 to decode—and understand—words with multiple syllables and morphemes.* Scholastic.

Moats, L. C., & Foorman, B. R. (2003). Measuring teachers' content knowledge of language and reading. *Annals of Dyslexia, 53*(1), 23–45. http://www.jstor.org/stable/23764733

Moore Partin, T. C., Robertson, R. E., Maggin, D. M., Oliver, R. M., & Wehby, J. H. (2010). Using teacher praise and opportunities to respond to promote appropriate student behavior. *Preventing School Failure: Alternative Education for Children and Youth, 54*(3), 172–178.

Moreno, R. (2004). Decreasing cognitive load for novice students: Effects of explanatory versus corrective feedback in discovery-based multimedia. *Instructional Science, 32*(1–2), 99–113.

NCS Pearson, Inc. (2018). *aimswebPlus development manual. AIMS web plus*

Nathan, R. G., & Stanovich, K. E. (1991). The causes and consequences of differences in reading fluency. *Theory Into Practice, 30*(3), 176–184.

National Center for Education Statistics. (2024). *National Assessment of Educational Progress (NAEP), 2024 reading assessment.*

National Center for Education Statistics. (2025). *2024 NAEP reading assessment: Results at grades 4 and 8 for the nation, states, and districts* (NCES 2024218) [Data set]. U.S. Department of Education, Institute of Education Sciences.

National Center on Intensive Intervention. (2024, December). *Using diagnostic data to inform intervention: Academic module* [PowerPoint slides]. https://intensiveintervention.org/sites/default/files/2024-12/diagnostic_data_acaddemic_module.pptx

National Council of Teachers of English, & International Reading Association. (2009). *Standards for the assessment of reading and writing* (Revised ed.). https://ncte.org/resources/standards/standards-for-the-assessment-of-reading-and-writing-revised-edition-2009/

National Institute of Child Health and Human Development. (2000). *Report of the National Reading Panel: Teaching children to read: Reports of the subgroups* (NIH Publication No. 00-4754). U.S. Department of Health and Human Services, National Institutes of Health.

Ness, M., & Miles, K. P. (2025). *Making words stick: A four-step instructional routine to power up orthographic mapping.* Scholastic.

95 Percent Group. (2023). *95 Phonics Screener for Intervention (95 PSI).* https://www.95percentgroup.com/products/95-phonics-screener-for-intervention-psi/

Parker, D. C., & Burns, M. K. (2014). Using the instructional level as a criterion to target reading interventions. *Reading & Writing Quarterly, 30*(1), 79–94.

Parker, D. C., Zaslofsky, A. F., Burns, M. K., Kanive, R., Hodgson, J., Scholin, S. E., & Klingbeil, D. A. (2015). A brief report of the diagnostic accuracy of oral reading fluency and reading inventory levels for reading failure risk among second- and third-grade students. *Reading & Writing Quarterly, 31*(1), 56–67.

Perfetti, C. A., & Hart, L. (2002). The lexical quality hypothesis. In L. Verhoeven, C. Elbro, & P. Reitsma (Eds.), *Precursors of functional literacy* (pp. 67–86). John Benjamins.

Powell-Smith, K. A., Good, R. H., III, Kaminski, R., & Wallin, J. (2021). *Acadience Reading Survey*. Voyager Sopris Learning.

Powell-Smith, K. A., Kaminski, R. A., & Good, R. H., III. (2021). *Acadience reading diagnostic: Comprehension, fluency, and oral language (CFOL)*. Acadience Learning Inc.

Simmons, D. C., Kuykendall, K., King, K., Cornachione, C., & Kameenui, E. J. (2000). Implementation of a schoolwide reading improvement model: "No one ever told us it would be this hard!". *Learning Disabilities Research & Practice, 15*(2), 92–100.

Simmons, D. C., Kame'enui, E. J., Good, R. H., III, Harn, B. A., Cole, C., & Braun, D. (2002). Building, implementing, and sustaining a beginning reading improvement model: Lessons learned school by school. In M. R. Shinn, H. M. Walker, & G. Stoner (Eds.), *Interventions for academic and behavior problems II: Preventive and remedial approaches* (pp. 537–569). National Association of School Psychologists.

Snow, C. E., Burns, M. S., & Griffin, P. (Eds.). (1998). *Preventing reading difficulties in young children*. National Academy Press.

Spencer, M., Quinn, J. M., & Wagner, R. K. (2014). Specific reading comprehension disability: Major problem, myth, or misnomer? *Learning Disabilities Research & Practice, 29*(1), 3–9.

Stahl, S. A., & Nagy, W. E. (2006). *Teaching word meanings* (1st ed.). Routledge.

Stecker, P. M., Fuch, L., & Fuchs, D. (2005). Using curriculum-based measurement to improve student achievement: Review of research. *Psychology in the Schools, 42*(8), 795–819.

Stephanie Stollar Consulting, LLC. (n.d.). *Reading Science Academy*. https://www.readingscienceacademy.com/

Sutherland, K. S., & Wehby, J. H. (2001). Exploring the relationship between increased opportunities to respond to academic requests and the academic and behavioral outcomes of students with EBD: A review. *Remedial and Special Education, 22*(2), 113–121.

Tilly, W. D., Reschly, D. J., & Grimes, J. (1999). Disability determination in problem-solving systems: Conceptual foundations and critical components. In D. J. Reschly, W. D. Tilly, & J. P. Grimes (Eds.), *Special education in transition: Functional assessment and noncategorical programming* (pp. 221–254). Sopris West.

Tindal, G. (2017). *Oral reading fluency: Outcomes from 30 years of research.* (Technical Report 1701). University of Oregon Center Behavioral Research and Teaching.

Torgesen, J. K. (2002). The prevention of reading difficulties. *Journal of School Psychology, 40*(1), 7–26.

Torgesen, J. K., & Burgess, S. R. (1998). Consistency of reading-related phonological processes throughout early childhood: Evidence from longitudinal-correlational and instructional studies. In J. L. Metsala & L. C. Ehri (Eds.), *Word recognition in beginning reading* (pp. 161–188). Lawrence Erlbaum Associates.

Toste, J. R., Filderman, M. J., Clemens, N. H., & Fry, E. (2025). Graph out loud: Pre-service teachers' data decisions and interpretations of CBM progress graphs. *Journal of Learning Disabilities, 58*(1), 33–45.

Truckenmiller, A., Coyne, M., Valentine, K. A., Moura, P., & Sarmiento, C. M. (2025, May 9). *Independent researcher review of commercial reading screening assessment suites May 2025.*

University of Oregon. (2021). Dynamic Indicators of Basic Early Literacy Skills (DIBELS®) (8th ed.). University of Oregon. https://dibels.uoregon.edu/

VanDerHeyden, A., & Burns, M. (2023). The instructional hierarchy: Connecting student learning and instruction. *Perspectives on Language and Literacy, 49*(1), 10–13.

VanDerHeyden, A. M., & Solomon, B. G. (2023). Valid outcomes for screening and progress monitoring: Fluency is superior to accuracy in curriculum-based measurement. *School Psychology, 38*(3), 160–172.

Winn, K. (Host). (2023, August 7). Universal screening for effective instruction with Renata Archie (S1 E6) [Audio podcast episode]. In *Reading Road Trip*. International Dyslexia Association Ontario. https://reading-roadtrip.castos.com/episodes/s1-e6-universal-screening-for-effective-instruction-with-renata-archie

Winn, K. (Host). (2024, August 26). Supporting gifted and advanced readers with Dr. Amanda Nickerson (S3 E9) [Audio podcast episode]. In *Reading Road Trip*. International Dyslexia Association Ontario. https://reading-roadtrip.castos.com/episodes/s3-e9-supporting-gifted-and-advanced-readers-with-dr-amanda-nickerson

Winn, K. (Host). (2024, September 2). The science of learning with Dr. Amanda VanDerHeyden (S3 E10) [Audio podcast episode]. In *Reading Road Trip*. International Dyslexia Association Ontario. https://reading-roadtrip.castos.com/episodes/s3-e10

Winn, K. (Host). (2024, January 29). Equity and literacy: Real talk with Kareem Weaver (S2 E5) [Audio podcast episode]. In *Reading Road Trip*. International Dyslexia Association Ontario. https://reading-roadtrip.castos.com/episodes/s2-e5-equity-and-literacy-real-talk-with-kareem-weaver

Zucker, T. A., & Cabell, S. Q. (2024). *Strive-for-five conversations: A framework that gets kids talking to accelerate their language comprehension & literacy*. Scholastic.

Index

K

L

M

N

O

P

Q